O. S.

POCKET ENC

BRITIS

STEAM RAILWAYS

OVER 100 COLOUR ILLUSTRATIONS

O. S. NOCK

hamlyn

An Hachette UK Company
www.hachette.co.uk

First published in Great Britain in 1983 by Blandford Press, Poole, Dorset

www.octopusbooks.co.uk

Published in 2009 by Bounty Books,
a division of Octopus Publishing Group Ltd
Carmelite House, 50 Victoria Embankment, London, EC4Y 0DZ

This edition published in 2018 by Hamlyn,
a division of Octopus Publishing Group Ltd

ISBN 978-0-7537-3285-4

A CIP catalogue record for this book is available from the British Library

Printed and bound in China

10 9 8 7 6 5 4 3 2 1

For this Hamlyn edition
Publisher: Lucy Pessell
Designer: Lisa Layton
Editor: Sarah Vaughan
Senior Production Manager: Peter Hunt

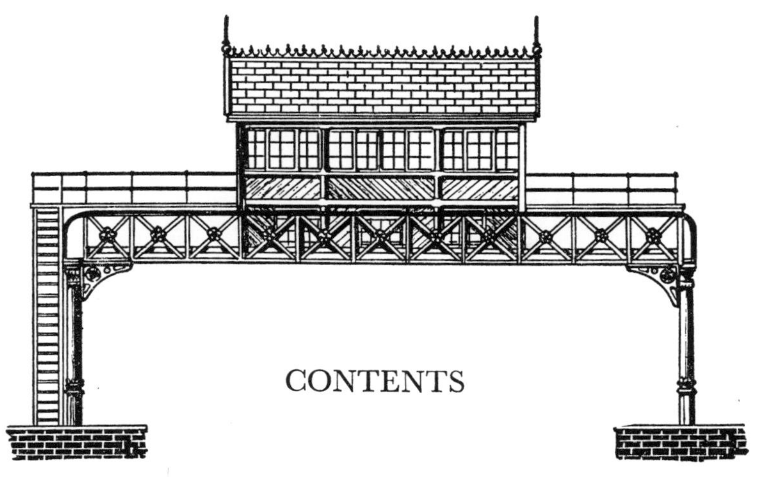

CONTENTS

Preface	5
Historical Introduction	7
The Colour Illustrations	13
Descriptions	109
Index	191

PREFACE

From the very inception of steam railways it was perhaps inevitable that the locomotive itself should form the centrepiece of popular interest. For it was the locomotive and its prowess that made possible the striking developments in social evolution in Great Britain that followed the building of railways.

In an earlier volume in this series the process of technical development in the design of locomotives was traced, and the artistic adornment of the machines themselves portrayed in 192 coloured illustrations; but while it was not possible in that first volume to picture more than a typical selection from the multifarious types that have run the rails in Great Britain, it was realized only too well that in these days interest in the steam railways is by no means confined to locomotives. The growth of the skilled and fascinating hobby of railway modelling has drawn the keen interest of many enthusiasts upon the design and embellishments of passenger carriages, while equally the desire to preserve, even if in no more than a miniature form, the authentic atmosphere of the old steam railways has emphasized the vast field of study represented by the semaphore signalling practice of the individual railways.

In preparing this book I have had once again the expert and delightful assistance of Charles Rickitt and his artists Clifford and Wendy Meadway.

I am grateful to British Railways for much valuable help in looking out drawings and photographs and to my one-time colleague in the Westinghouse Brake and Signal Company, Douglas Wilkinson, whose sketches of picturesque semaphore signal arrangements have formed the basis of some of the coloured illustrations. I am also indebted to John H. Scholes, Curator of Historical Relics, British Railways Board, for his help in connection with the coats of arms.

Lastly, as always, my special thanks are due to Olivia, my wife, for her advice and help, and for typing the MSS.

O. S. Nock

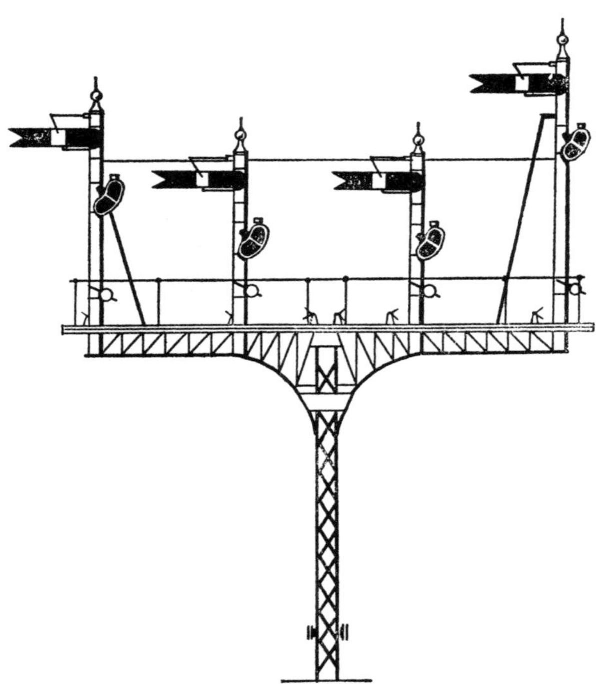

HISTORICAL INTRODUCTION

In the earlier volume of this series, *The Pocket Encyclopaedia of British Steam Locomotives*, the origins and development of this great invention were described, and its influence upon the social evolution of this country emphasised. In the rapid development of railways the steam locomotive, which alone made possible the tremendous nineteenth-century speed-up in communications, naturally claimed most of the limelight. Those who began to take more than a passing interest in this new mode of travel were naturally drawn to the gaily painted machines that trundled the early trains along, and they were fascinated by the manifestations of power evidenced by the puffing of the exhaust, the escape of steam through the safety valves; and those early enthusiasts realized that steam locomotives had for them an emotional as well as a scientific appeal.

In this second volume a further selection of historical steam locomotives are illustrated in colour, including a few specially adorned for great occasions like the London and North Western compounds *Greater Britain* and *Queen Empress*, gorgeously painted in honour of the Diamond Jubilee of Queen Victoria's reign. But in this book other aspects of the British steam railways are noticed. There is, for example, the development in carriage design. This is a deeply interesting subject which provides a reflection upon social conditions of the times, and how the travel habit gradually spread and led to a greatly improved standard of comfort for people travelling at the very lowest fares. The earliest first class carriages were built exactly in the style of a stagecoach. Those who had travelled 'inside' on the old mail coaches expected, and received, the same standards of comfort on the new railways. The stage coach builders of old applied their craft to the building of first class carriages for the railways, and whereas the stage coaches had but a single compartment the new railway carriages had at least three.

Travel in separate compartments was considered the normal standard of luxury, and it is a form of carriage design that has persisted throughout the steam railway age in this country. Just as on the old stage coaches many passengers had to travel outside and brave the elements in bad weather, so, on the earliest railways, open carriages were provided for second and third class passengers. The 'seconds' had a canopy over the top, but were completely open at the sides, while the thirds were just open trucks. At first no one thought anything of it. Many people had always travelled 'outside', some for very long distances. But as the travel habit began to grow, so there grew also an agitation for better carriages for the third class passengers. By the end of the eighteen-thirties railway speed was passing far beyond the fastest of mail coaches on the road; while on the road the outside passengers had only the elements to brave, on railways there were smuts, cinders, and smoke from the engines – not to mention the unpleasant conditions when passing through the tunnels.

In 1844 when W. E. Gladstone was President of the Board of Trade, the celebrated 'Regulation of Railways Act' was passed by Parliament, and all railways were bound by law to provide covered-in carriages for third class passengers at the statutory fare of one penny per mile. Some of the early rolling stock used to comply with this regulation was forbidding in the extreme, and consisted of little more than closed-in boxes, with the merest slits to provide light and ventilation. Furthermore some of the railway companies ran the so-called 'Parliamentary' trains only at night, when their presence and slow progress would be least likely to delay first class and mail traffic. Although things became vastly better for the third class passenger as railway travel increased, on some suburban lines in London third class carriages with bare boards for seats survived even until the nineteen-thirties.

The book illustrates the development of passenger carriages from these primitive and spartan types to the first introduction of dining and sleeping cars, and to the gradual superseding of four- and six-wheeled stock by smooth-riding bogie coaches. At the same time there have been many interesting vehicles that were not available to the general public, yet becoming familiar to regular travellers. Of these the Travelling Post Office vans must be specially mentioned, most of which were equipped with apparatus for picking up and dropping mail bags at full speed. It is interesting to recall that this apparatus was introduced as long ago as 1838 on the Grand Junction Railway – later a section of the London and North Western Railway. The network of railway postal services worked by T.P.O. vans reached its zenith shortly after World War I, and on some of the more important services mail bags would be picked up and set down at a great number of intermediate stations en route, where the train itself did not stop.

Today, however, mail bag exchange on the T.P.O. trains is on a very much reduced scale. The postal authorities now find it more convenient to concentrate mail traffic at a few large centres and distribute from such centres by road, than to collect and deliver small consignments at wayside stations. The Midland route from Bristol to the north is a case in point. At one time mail bags were exchanged at small stations like Wickwar and Charfield, but now there is no mail bag exchange at speed on the Midland T.P.O.; all the traffic is dealt with at the large stopping stations, such as Gloucester and Birmingham. Thus a very interesting and picturesque aspect of railway working is tending to disappear.

In Great Britain the vehicles used on passenger trains have mostly been as distinctive and colourful as the locomotives themselves. In this respect British railways have always stood out distinctly from the steam railways on the continent of Europe, which for the most part were uniformly drab in outward appearance. The technique of railway carriage building, as in the physical style of the compartments had its origins in coaching days. The indigenous materials familiar to the coach builders of old were used in railway vehicles, and until well into the twentieth century the bodies of lengthy main line corridor carriages were constructed in wood, even though steel was coming into general use for the underframing. The use of timber for the bodies perpetuated a picturesque form of construction in which the sides and ends were elaborately panelled; and with that same pride of finish, that was manifested in the gay liveries applied to locomotives, carriages were not only beautifully finished so far as basic painting was concerned, but were elaborately lined out, and usually adorned with the company's coat of arms. Some highly decorative examples of railway heraldry are illustrated in this book, and points about the individual designs are discussed in the descriptive matter relating to particular illustrations.

The railways of this country, in their choice of colour schemes, displayed a rare artistic taste in adopting combinations of locomotive and carriage liveries that blended harmoniously together. Only three companies painted engines and coaches the same colour, yet in other cases the combinations were not only pleasing in themselves, but were suited to those instances where on long through runs a change of locomotive introduced no jarring note in colour combinations. In this book the illustrations have in many cases been grouped so as to show contemporary locomotive and carriage styles together, such as the black engines, and chocolate and white coaches of the London and North Western; the beautiful green, and varnished teak of the Great Northern, and the crimson-lake of both engines and carriages on the Midland. On all routes to Scotland harmony continued when the trains crossed the border, and the Midland trains were taken forward from Carlisle on one route by the rich brown engines of the North British, or on the other by the handsome dark green engines of the Glasgow and South Western. On the West Coast Route the blue Caledonians were natural successors to the black North Westerns.

Perhaps the most remarkably colourful effects were to be seen on the Highland Railway where it was not unusual to find through carriages from all three Anglo-Scottish routes from London marshalled in the same train from Perth to Inverness: chocolate and white North Western; crimson-lake Midland, and varnished teak Great Northern, interspersed with some of the local Highland green carriages, maybe a travelling post-office van, and hauled by a green Highland engine. The soft moss-green of the Highland engines blended remarkably well with the harlequin effects along the trains themselves, and might almost have been chosen for the very purpose!

Another phase in the evolution of railways that recalls a step in the gradual development of transport facilities in this country is represented by a group of four rail motor cars illustrated in this book. Early in the present century railways were already feeling the effects of high costs involved in working branch lines where traffic was light; and to reduce operating costs the conventional locomotive and carriage combination was replaced by very picturesque little combined units, in which a tiny locomotive was mounted on the main frames of a bogie coach. There were very few British railways that did not try this expedient, and in days when public transport by road in country districts consisted of nothing larger or faster than one-horse buses these rail motor cars filled a useful, if short-lived niche. They were rather slow; but then branch line services were generally slow in years before World War I.

The signals require a special word of commendation. The actual semaphores depicted in the coloured illustrations in this book form no more than the outward and visible signs of the great edifice of safety regulations, and ingenious mechanism that had been built up in the course of more than a hundred years of railway operation in this country. Travel at speeds of 80 m.p.h. or more is a common experience of countless persons today who drive, or ride in modern motor cars; and while road signs and traffic lights are becoming more frequent than they used to be the road user may sometimes be puzzled by the elaborate methods of signalling that are used on railways, when traffic does not appear to be so intense as on many a modern highway, and certainly travelling at no higher speeds. This is no place to discuss the relative merits, in the social conditions of today, of road and railway travel. Instead it is necessary to look back into the nineteenth century and to the first years of the present century, when railways were incomparably the fastest means of travel known to man.

Fundamentally the whole art of signalling on railways is linked up with the distances in which a train can be stopped. Exactly the same principles are naturally being used in connection with road traffic. On an ordinary road a motorist needs no more than 100 yards warning of a 'HALT SIGN' or traffic lights ahead; but on the motorways, where the fastest vehicles may be travelling at 100 m.p.h. or more, the first advice of junctions or changes in road conditions is given a mile in advance. On railways, even with the most modern of appliances, the process of braking steel wheels, running on smooth steel rails, must necessarily be more gradual than with a road vehicle; nor would very rapid deceleration be accepted as part of the usual standards of railway comfort. Signals were erected to give drivers ample warning that a stop or a deceleration was necessary, and at the same time the highly specialized science of interlocking was built up, whereby it was rendered a physical impossibility for a signalman to set points, or lower signals in such a way as to cause a collision at a junction. There did, of course, remain certain loop-holes, where a man could, in a moment of forgetfulness, omit to carry out a point of procedure in the regulations. The human element could still enter into things – albeit to a very limited extent; nevertheless it was a policy on the part of many railway administrations to sustain the high sense of responsibility manifested by the very great majority of all railwaymen concerned with the running of the trains. The wonderful safety record of the British railways in steam days – incomparably the finest in the world – provided ample justification for this policy.

As with locomotive and carriage design, and in the distinctive liveries, the old steam railways of Great Britain developed some very distinctive patterns of semaphore signals, and some of these are shown among the coloured illustrations in this book. While the basic semaphore indications were the same the details differed widely. But in the devices used for subsidiary movements individuality ran riot, and it has not been possible to illustrate more than a few of the varied styles that were once used. Another feature that contributed greatly to the picturesque aspects of the steam railways was the vast multiplicity of semaphore arms to be seen in the approaches to large stations. This was due to the need, in former days, of having a separate arm for each alternative route. In later years, even with semaphore arms, such elaboration was obviated by the use of route indicators; but the development of a really satisfactory form, that could be read and recognized equally well by day or night was a lengthy process, and one that was not finally solved until the nineteen-thirties, by which time the semaphore signal was definitely, if gradually, on the way out.

A full description of the colour illustrations which follow appears between pages 109-190

1 **Richard Trevithick's locomotive, 1804**; winner of the Pne-y-daren prize.

2 **Cauldron Wagon**; used on early railways for transport of coal. From these were developed the first third-class carriages.

3 **First class carriage "Traveller"**; Liverpool and Manchester Railway.

4 **Third class carriage**; Liverpool and Manchester Railway.

5 **First class carriage**; North Union Railway.

6 **Tri-composite four-wheeler of Monmouthshire Railway design**; Great Western Railway.

7 **Stirling 7 ft 7 in. 2–2–2**; Great Northern Railway. 1886 design.

8 **Four-wheeled brake-third carriage**; Great Northern Railway.

9 **Coniston branch 2–2–2 tank engine**; Furness Railway. Built 1866.

10 **Sir James Ramsden's Inspection Car**; Furness Railway.

11 **Suburban Tank Engine**; London, Chatham and Dover Railway.

12 **The celebrated 4–2–2 single No. 123**; Caledonian Railway. Built 1886.

13 **Rebuilt Cudworth 2–4–0 express locomotive**; South Eastern Railway.

14 **Midland and Great Northern Joint Railway**; 2–4–0 passenger engine.

15 **London Suburban Carriage**; Midland Railway.

16 **Second-class Suburban Carriage**; Great Eastern Railway.

17 **Local Train Carriage**; Great Western Railway.

18 **Four-wheeled Coach**; North London Railway.

19 **Webb eight-wheeled Radial Coach**; London and North Western Railway.

20 **T. G. Clayton's twelve-wheeled "brake-third"**; Midland Railway.

21 **Broad gauge composite carriage**; Great Western Railway.

22 **Boat Train six-wheeler**; South Eastern Railway.

23 **London and North Western Railway**; coat of arms.

24 **Midland Railway**; coat of arms.

25 **Lancashire and Yorkshire Railway**; coat of arms.

26 **North London Railway**; coat of arms.

27 **The** *Greater Britain* **engine**; London and North Western Railway, built 1891.

28 **West Coast Joint Stock Coach.**

29 **Diamond Jubilee celebration engine** *Queen Empress*; London and North Western Railway, 1897.

30 **One of the first dining cars**; London and North Western Railway, built 1889.

31 **Six-coupled 0–6–0 mineral engine**; North Eastern Railway, originally built 1866.

32 **Kirtley 2–4–0 No. 158A**; Midland Railway.

33 **Caledonian mixed traffic 2–4–0**; built 1877.

34 **"River" class 2–4–0** *Teign*; Great Western Railway.

35 **East Coast Joint Stock Sleeping Car.**

36 **Llandudno Club Carriage**; London and North Western Railway.

37 **Morecambe Club Carriage**; Midland Railway.

38 **Ocean Liner Sleeping Car**; London and South Western Railway.

39 **Caledonian Railway**; coat of arms.

40 **North British Railway**; coat of arms.

41 Highland Railway; coat of arms.

42 **Glasgow and South Western Railway**; coat of arms.

43 **Picnic Saloon**; London and North Western Railway.

44 **Chariot-ended, first class carriage**; Highland Railway.

45 **Composite four-wheeled carriage**; Somerset and Dorset Joint Railway.

46 **Family Saloon**; London, Chatham and Dover Railway.

47 **"L" class 4–4–0 locomotive**; South Eastern and Chatham Railway, built 1914.

48 **A Continental Boat Train Carriage**; South Eastern and Chatham Railway.

49 **Drummond's 4-cylinder "double-single" engine No. 720**; London and South Western Railway, built 1897, at first with smaller boiler.

50 **Main-line non-corridor carriage**; London and South Western Railway.

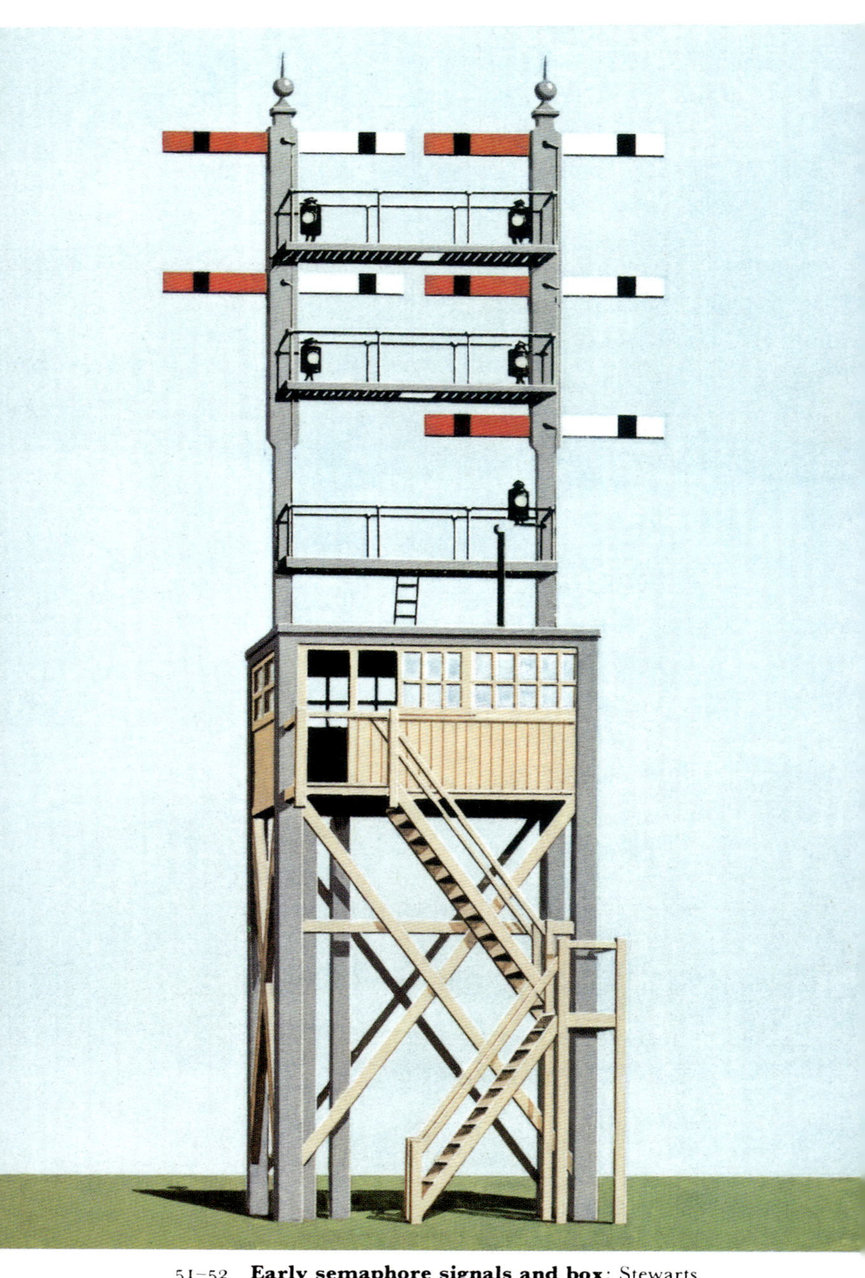

51–52 **Early semaphore signals and box**; Stewarts Lane Junction.

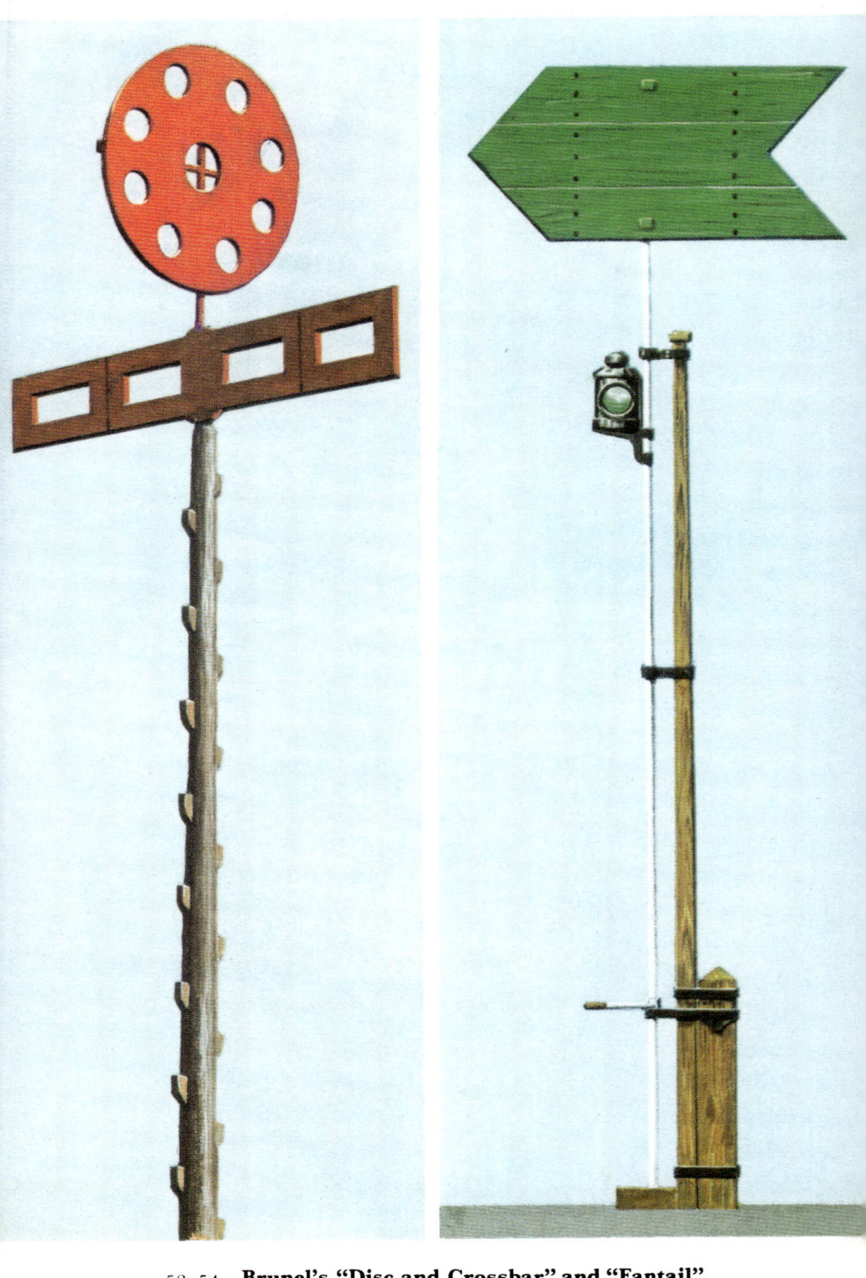

53–54 **Brunel's "Disc and Crossbar" and "Fantail" signals**; Great Western Railway.

55 **West Coast Joint Stock**; coat of arms.

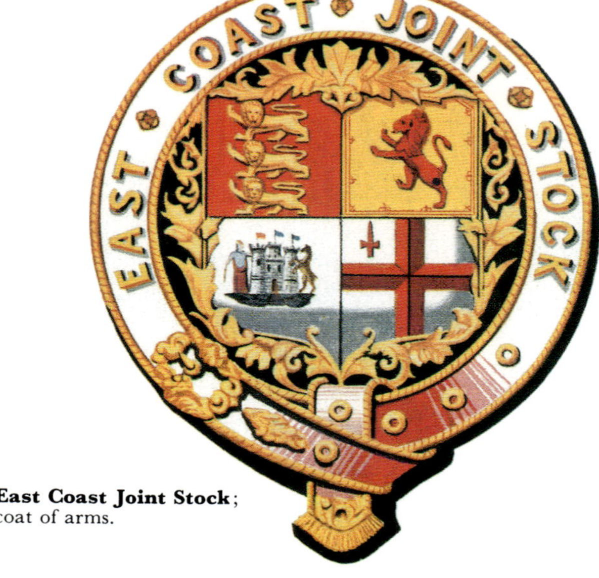

East Coast Joint Stock; coat of arms.

57 **The Royal Mail coat of arms**; used on Travelling Post Offices.

58 **Great North of Scotland Railway**; coat of arms.

59 **The "1020" class 4-4-0 locomotive**; Great Central Railway, built 1901.

60 **Vestibuled clerestory carriage**; Great Central Railway.

61 **Ivatt 4–2–2 locomotive, 1898**; Great Northern Railway.

62 **Clerestory brake-composite carriage**; Great Northern Railway.

63 **12-wheeled dining car**; West Coast Joint Stock.

64 **Third class dining car**; Midland Railway.

65 **Bow-ended elliptical-roofed dining car**; Great Northern Railway.

66 **Composite 70 ft dining car**; Great Western Railway.

67 **Hughes 4–6–4 tank engine**; London, Midland and Scottish Railway, built 1924.

68 **Adams 0–6–2 radial tank engine**; North Staffordshire Railway, built 1903.

69 **4–6–2 Express tank engine**; London and North Western Railway, built 1910.

70 **0–4–4 Passenger tank engine**; Midland Railway. introduced in 1875.

71 **Great Northern Railway**; coat of arms.

72 **Great Eastern Railway**; coat of arms.

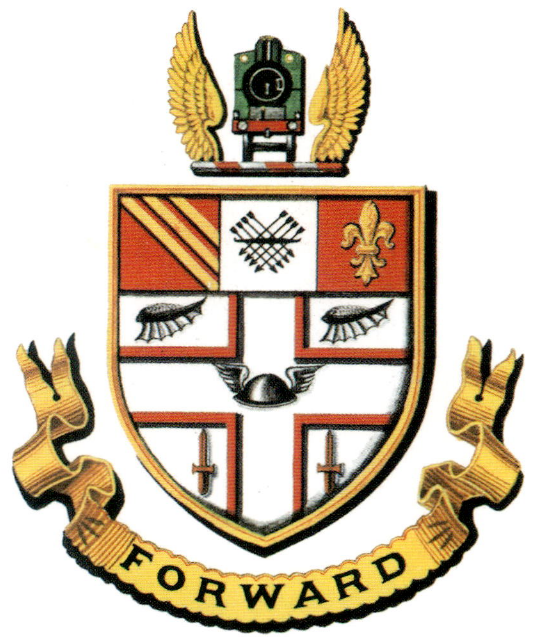

73 **Great Central Railway**; coat of arms.

4 **North Eastern Railway**; coat of arms.

75 **Webb Four-cylinder compound 4–4–0**; London and North Western Railway, of 1901 design.

76 **45 ft Corridor brake-first**; West Coast Joint Stock.

77 **"Duke of Cornwall" class 4-4-0 engine**; Great Western Railway, 1895 design.

78 **Narrow-gauge clerestory coach**; Great Western Railway.

79 **6 ft "Castle" class 4-6-0 of 1917**; Highland Railway.

80 **Composite Corridor Carriage**; Highland Railway.

81 **"Scott" class 4–4–0 locomotive**; North British Railway, 1914 design.

82 **Non-corridor first class carriage**; North British Railway.

83 **0–6–4 Passenger tank engine**; Midland Railway 1907 design.

84 **Pickersgill 4–6–2 tank engine**; Caledonian Railway, 1917 design.

85 **Robinson's 4–6–2 passenger tank engine**; Great Central Railway, built 1910.

86 **Reid 4–4–2 tank engine**; North British Railway, 1915 design.

87 **Dynamometer Car**; Great Western Railway.

88 **North Eastern Railway**; dynamometer car in L.N.E.R. livery.

89 **Dynamometer Car of 1908**; London and North Western Railway.

90 **A Modern Dynamometer Car;** London Midland and Scottish Railway No. 3, of 1948.

91 **London and South Western Railway**; coat of arms.

92 **South Eastern Railway**; coat of arms.

93 **London Chatham and Dover Railway**; coat of arms.

94 **London Brighton and South Coast Railway**; coat of arms.

95 **Travelling Post Office Van**; Highland Railway.

96 **Combined T.P.O. and passenger coach**; Great Western Railway.

97 **Tri-composite corridor brake coach**; South Eastern and Chatham Railway.

98 **Tri-composite lavatory carriage**; Cambrian Railways.

99 **"Experiment" class 4–6–0 locomotive**; London and North Western Railway, 1905.

100 **57 ft Corridor composite carriage**; London and North Western Railway.

101 **A "Barochan" class 4–6–0**; Caledonian Railway, 1906.

102 **A "Grampian" corridor carriage**; Caledonian Railway.

103 **Great Eastern Semaphore Signal.**

104 **Caledonian Semaphore Signal.**

105 **North Eastern Semaphore Signal.**

106 **Great Northern centre-balanced semaphore signal.**

107 **Ocean Mail Stowage Van**; Great Western Railway.

108 **Six-wheeled Travelling Post Office**; Great Northern Railway.

109 **T.P.O. Van for the Postal "Special"**; West Coast Joint Stock.

110 **Six-wheeled Travelling Post Office**; Midland Railway.

111 **Robinson's 0–6–0 Goods engine**; Great Central Railway.

112 **Composite slip-brake carriage**; Great Central Railway.

113 **Bogie third-class carriage**; London Brighton and South Coast Railway.

114 **L. Billinton's 2–6–0 express goods engine**; London Brighton and South Coast Railway.

115 **Rebuilt non-superheater 4–4–0, No. 2 class**; Midland Railway.

116 **David Bain's design of "brake-first"**; Midland Railway.

117 **Wilson Worsdell's "V" class "Atlantic"**; North Eastern Railway.

118 **Elliptical-roofed corridor carriage**; North Eastern Railway.

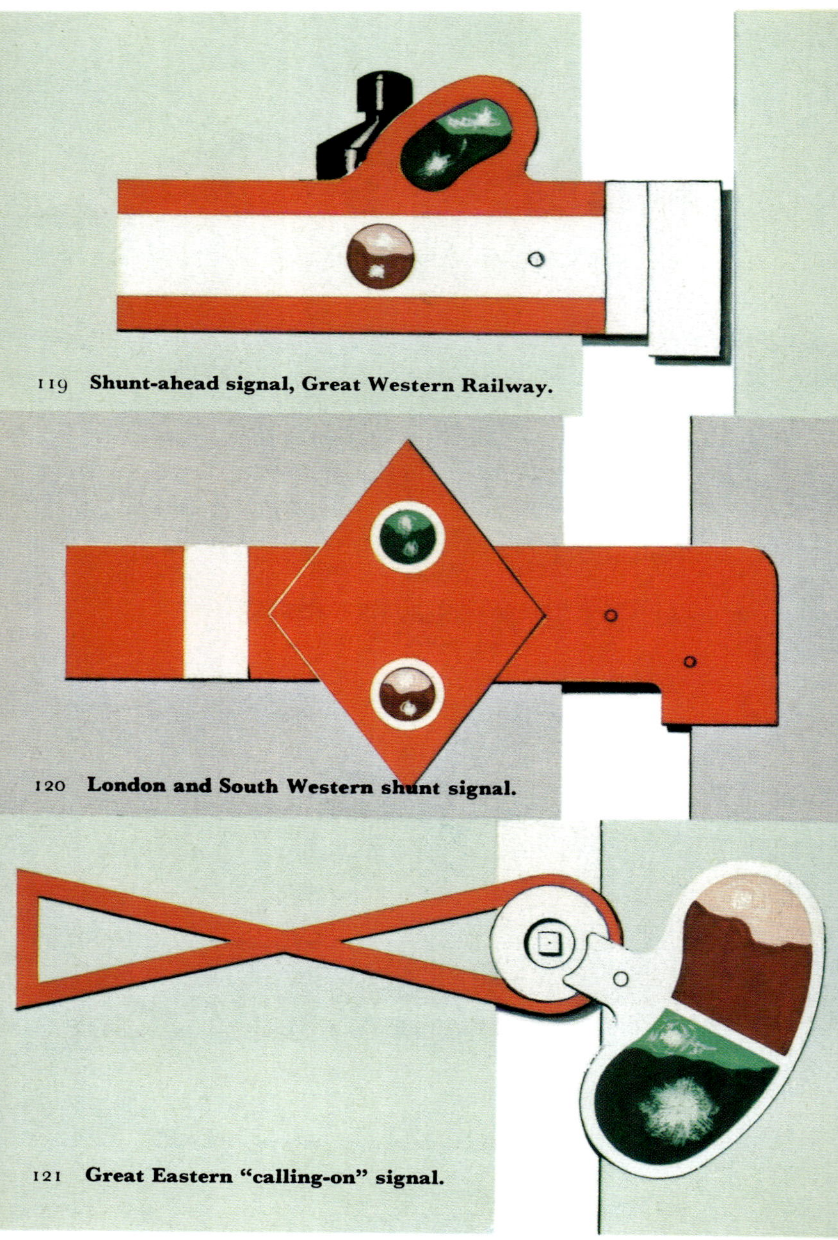

119 **Shunt-ahead signal, Great Western Railway.**

120 **London and South Western shunt signal.**

121 **Great Eastern "calling-on" signal.**

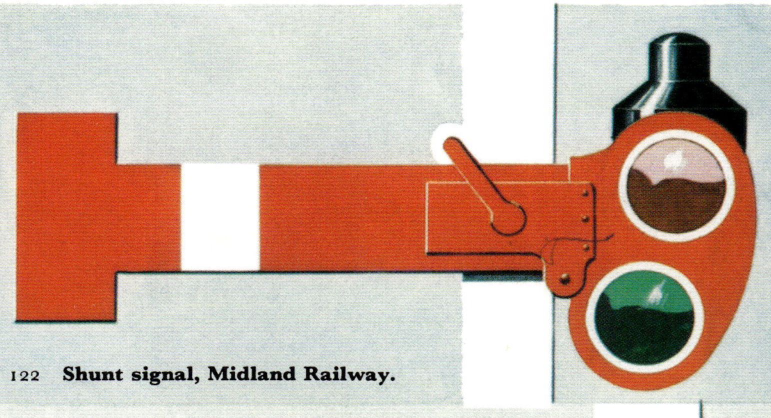

122 **Shunt signal, Midland Railway.**

123 **Subsidiary signal, London Brighton and South Coast Railway.**

124 **"Backing" signal, Great Western Railway.**

125 **Taff Vale Railway**; coat of arms.

126 **Rhymney Railway**; coat of arms.

127 **Cambrian Railways**; coat of arms.

128 **Festiniog Railway**; coat of arms.

129 **Ocean Special Saloon**; Great Western Railway.

130 **David Bain's design of Royal Saloon**; Midland Railway.

131 **Saloon Carriage, No. 1**; Furness Railway.

132 **Open Saloon third class**; Great Central Railway.

133 **Corridor third class carriage**; Great Eastern Railway.

134 **Twelve-wheeled dining car**; Midland Anglo-Scottish Joint stock.

135 **Non-corridor bogie composite carriage**; Somerset and Dorset Joint Railway.

136 **Open "brake-third" corridor carriage**; Lancashire and Yorkshire Railway.

137 **Churchward's "County" class 4-4-0 of 1904**; Great Western Railway.

138 **70 ft Corridor Carriage, 1908 design**; Great Western Railway.

139 **Hawksworth's "County" class 4–6–0 of 1945**; Great Western Railway.

140 **Bow-ended corridor carriage of 1947**; Great Western Railway.

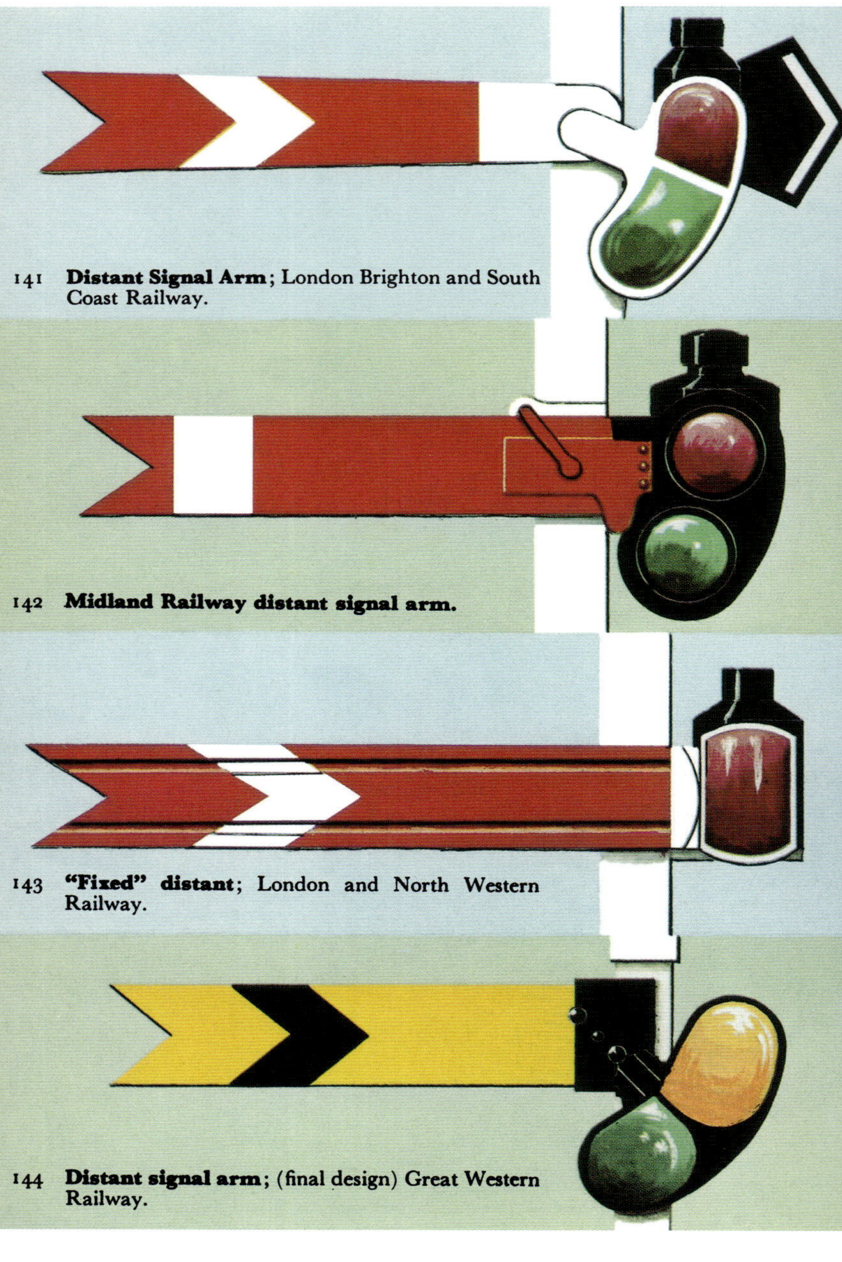

141 **Distant Signal Arm**; London Brighton and South Coast Railway.

142 **Midland Railway distant signal arm.**

143 **"Fixed" distant**; London and North Western Railway.

144 **Distant signal arm**; (final design) Great Western Railway.

145
Tall Semaphore Signal, with co-acting lower arms; Great Western Railway

146
Tall Semaphore Signals, for 4-track lines; London and North Western Railway.

147 **Large-boilered "Claughton" class 4–6–0**; London Midland and Scottish Railway.

148 **Open-third saloon carriage**; London Midland and Scottish Railway.

149 **Rebuilt "Lord Nelson" class 4–6–0**; Southern Railway.

150 **Standard corridor coach**; Bulleid era, Southern Railway.

151 **Furness Railway**; rail motor and trailer.

152 **Rail Motor, Edgware branch**; Great Northern Railway.

153 **Lancashire and Yorkshire rail motor.**

154 **70 ft rail motor coach**; Great Western Railway.

155 *Maid of Morven* **observation car**; Caledonian Railway.

156 **Waverley Route sleeping car**; M. & N.B. joint Scotch stock.

157 **The Coronation beaver-tail observation car**; London and North Eastern Railway, 1937.

158 **The "Centenary Riviera" stock**; Great Western Railway, 1935.

159 **The first Gresley streamlined Pacific**; No. 2509 *Silver Link*, built 1935.

160 **2-car articulated coach set**; "Silver Jubilee" train, London and North Eastern Railway, 1935.

161 **Stanier streamlined Pacific**; in "red" livery as used for these engines from 1939 on the L.M.S.R.

162 **"Coronation Scot" coach**; for New York World's Fair, 1939.

163 **Great Western Railway**; coat of arms.

164 **London Midland and Scottish Railway**; coat of arms.

165 **London and North Eastern Railway**; coat of arms.

166 **The Pullman coat of arms.**

167 **E. Thompson's "A2" class Pacific**; London and North Eastern Railway, 1947.

168 **Bulleid's Austerity 0–6–0 goods**; Class "Q1" Southern Railway.

169 **"Schools" class 4–4–0 in wartime livery**; Southern Railway.

170 **L.M.S.R. Class "5" 4–6–0**; with Caprotti valve gear.

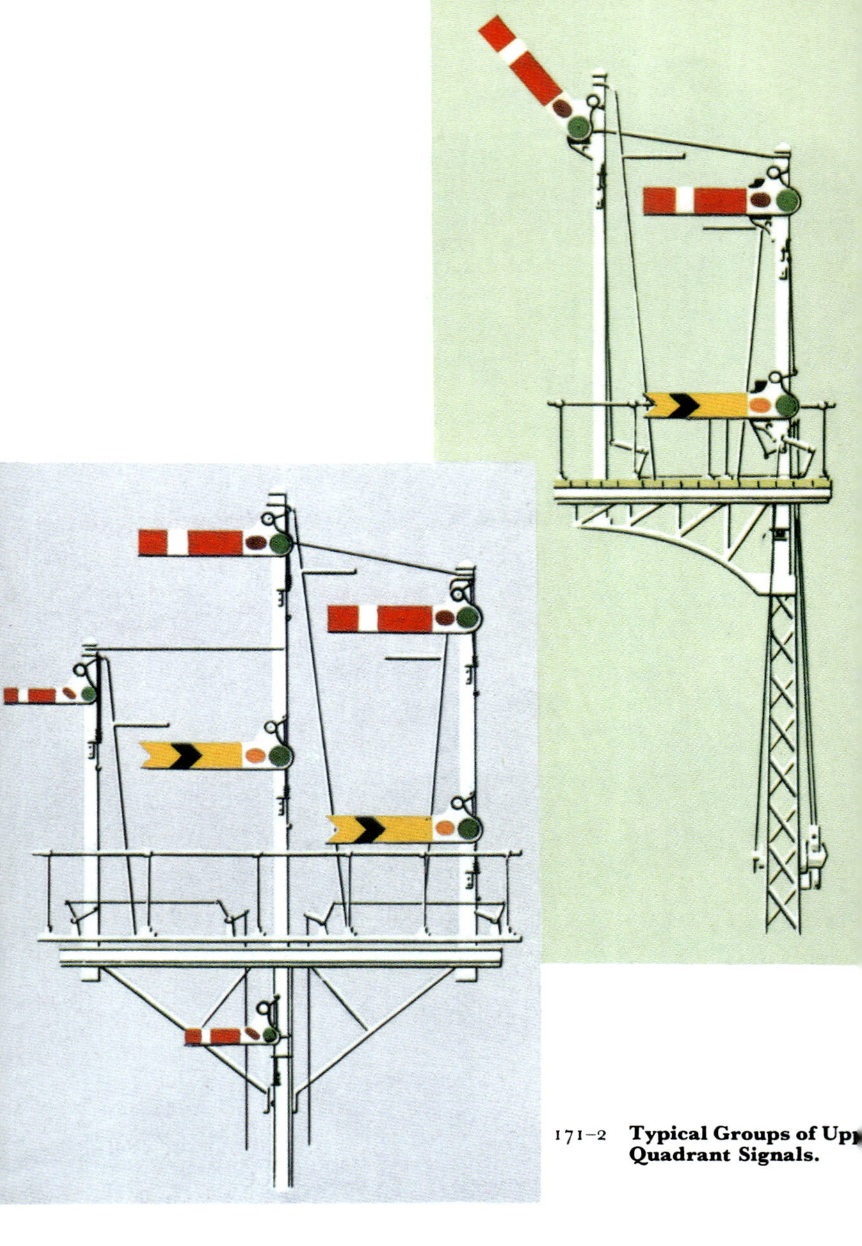

171–2 **Typical Groups of Up
Quadrant Signals.**

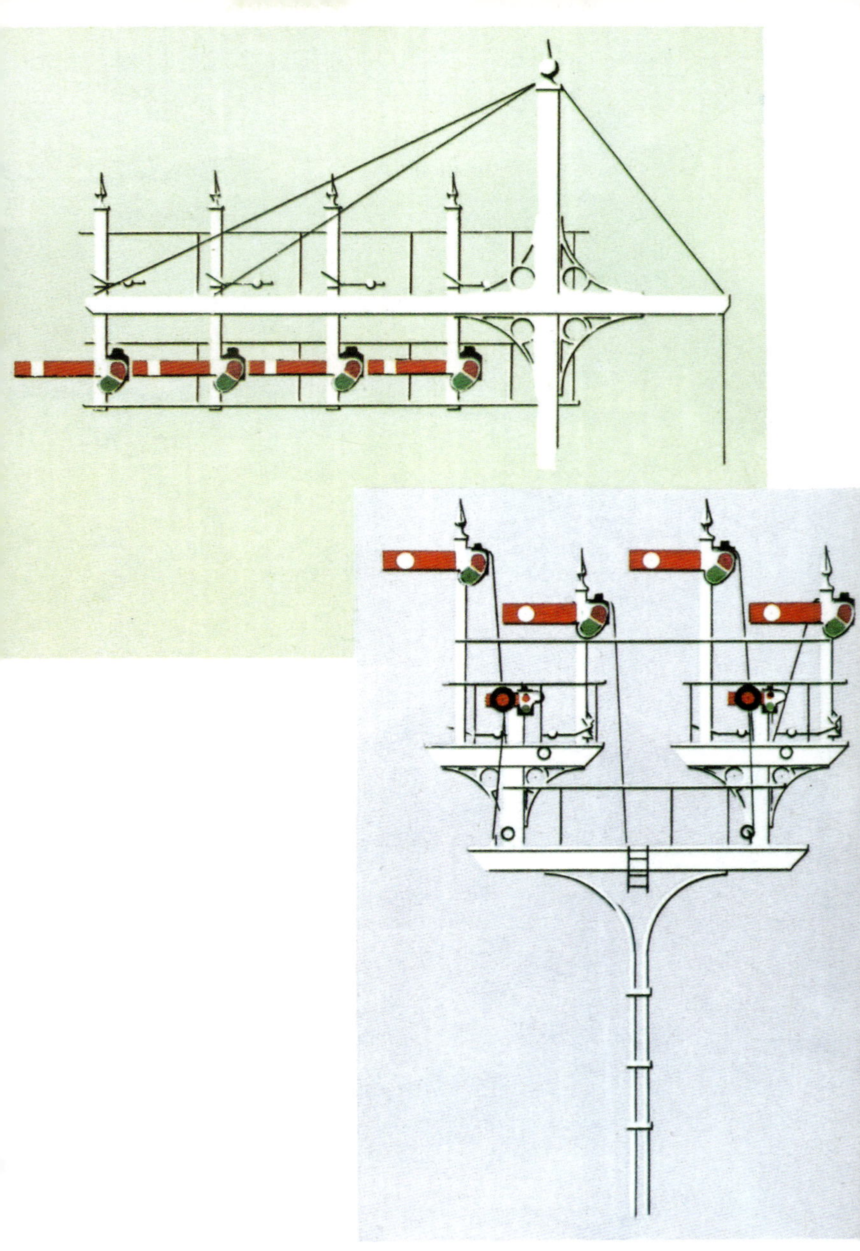

173–4 **Typical Groups of Semaphore Signals**; South Eastern and Chatham Railway.

175 **Fowler 2-6-4 fast passenger tank engine**; London Midland and Scottish Railway.

176 **Thompson's 2-6-4 tank engine, Class "L1" for mixed traffic**; London and North Eastern Railway.

177 **Heavy Mineral 2–8–2 tank engine**; "72XX" class Great Western Railway.

178 **"BR4" Standard 2–6–4 tank engine**; British Railways.

179 **Furness Railway**; coat of arms.

180 **Somerset and Dorset Joint Railway**; coat of arms.

Hull and Barnsley Railway;
coat of arms.

82 **North Staffordshire Railway**;
coat of arms.

183 **The** *Princess Elizabeth* **engine, in black**; British Railways London Midland Region.

184 **"Merchant Navy" class 4–6–2 in standard blue**; British Railways, Southern Region.

185 **A Gresley "A3" Pacific in experimental dark blue**; British Railways, Eastern and North Eastern Regions.

186 **A "Castle" class 4–6–0 in experimental light green**; British Railways Western Region.

187 **Double-chimneyed "King" class 4–6–0**; British Railways, Western Region.

188 **Standard main line coaching stock**; in first style of painting, British Railways.

189 **Rebuilt "Royal Scot" 4–6–0 in "standard" green**; British Railways.

190 **Standard main line coaching stock, with Commonwealth bogies**; British Railways.

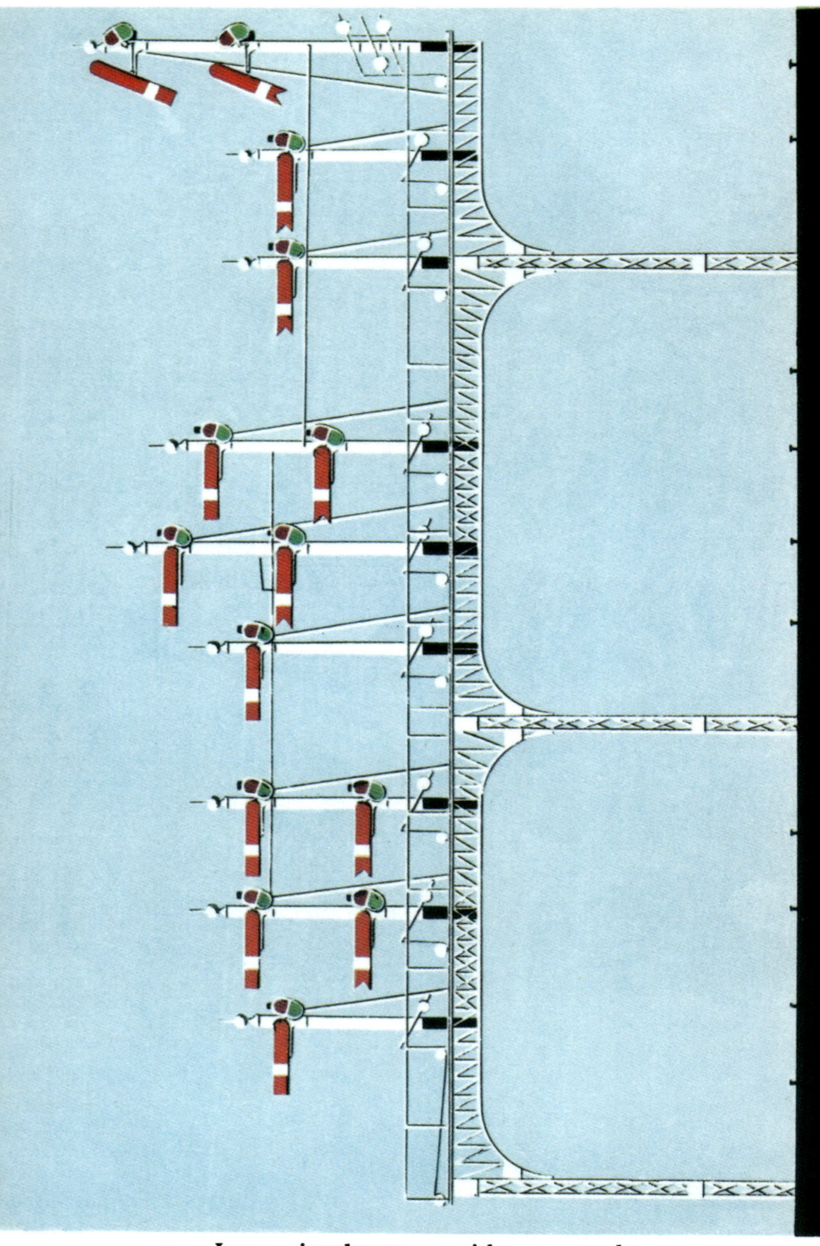

191 **Large signal gantry, with somersault type arms**; Great Northern Railway.

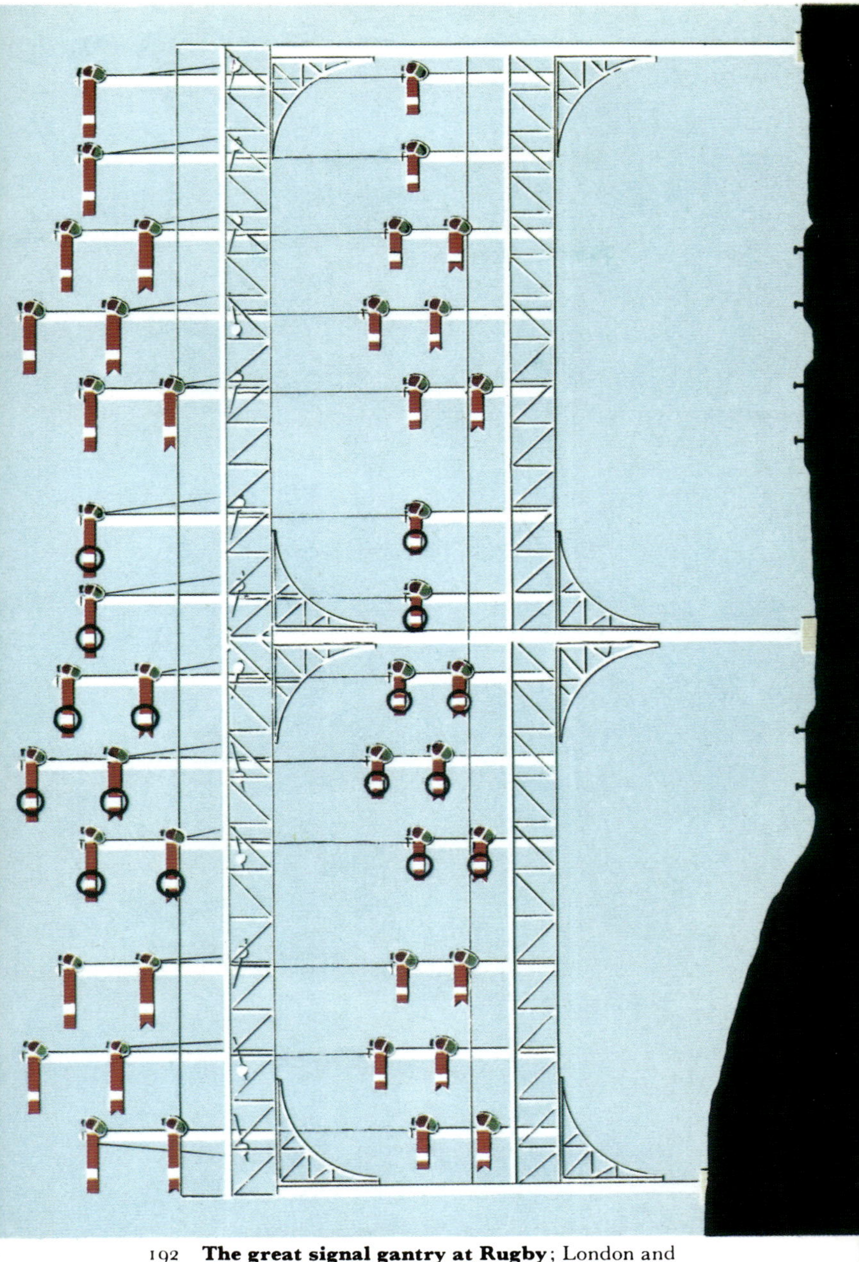

192 **The great signal gantry at Rugby**; London and North Western Railway.

193 **"BR6" Pacific "Clan" class**; British Railways.

194 **"BR9" 2–10–0 with Franco-Crosti boiler**; British Railways.

1 **Richard Trevithick's locomotive, 1804;** winner of the Pen-y-daren prize. At one time there was much controversy over the question of who was the true originator of steam railways. While it was certain that George Stephenson built the first public railway in 1825, and had the vision and the keen practical outlook to set the railway industry firmly on its way, there were many men before him who had been experimenting with steam engines – not necessarily for the purpose of locomotion. Of these none was more daring in his ideas nor achieved a greater measure of success than the great Cornish mining engineer, Richard Trevithick. Yet his greatest triumph with steam locomotives was secured not in Cornwall but in Wales. Samuel Homfray, a prominent iron-master, was greatly interested in Trevithick's work and in 1804 proposed to use a steam locomotive on the 'plate-way' that existed from his two works at Pen-y-daren to the canal at Abercynon. One of his fellow iron-masters challenged him, with a bet of 500 guineas, that the locomotive would not haul a load of 10 tons over that distance. Trevithick entered into the spirit of the wager with tremendous enthusiasm, and when the appointed day came they carried 10 tons of iron, 5 wagons and 70 men riding on them the whole way. It is true that they took 4 hr. 5 min. to do the journey of 9 miles; but apparently the suitability of the line had been surveyed less carefully than the locomotive had been prepared, and they had to stop several times to cut down trees that blocked the way, and at one point some rocks had to be removed! Nevertheless, on clear sections the engine travelled at 5 m.p.h. and Homfray won his bet. Trevithick's locomotive contained many imperfections, and a vast amount of experimenting had to be done with steam between the year 1804 and Robert Stephenson's triumph with the *Rocket* at Rainhill, in 1829. But the Pen-y-daren locomotive can be set down as the very first to haul a good load successfully.

2 **Cauldron Wagons;** early railways. On the ever-famous journey of Trevithick's locomotive along the 9 miles of the Pen-y-daren 'plate-way', 70 men were carried, partly to make up the load, and equally to share in the excitements and triumphs of the day. One can imagine that none of them minded any discomfort or inconvenience from riding in trucks designed for conveyance of coal or iron. It was the same at the opening of the Stockton and Darlington Railway in 1825. That line, the first public railway in the world, was built primarily for the conveyance of coal, and for that the cauldron wagons were the standard form of vehicle. The passenger services were operated by single vehicles drawn by a horse, and these coaches were in the style of a stage coach. But as the popularity of the railway increased, and more and more people of humble means wanted to travel, accommodation was provided for them in open trucks. On the Stockton and Darlington Railway the cauldron wagons were adapted for the purpose, and as time went on special carriages for passengers paying the lowest fares were built. These 'carriages' were nothing more than enlarged wagons, with nothing in the way of seats or protection from the weather. It sounds a little crude; but passengers of the lowest orders expected no different in those early days. Hitherto, if such folk had required to make a journey there had been nothing for it but to walk!

3 **First-class carriage, 'Traveller';** Liverpool and Manchester Railway. While the Stockton and Darlington Railway, opened in 1825, was the first public railway, the Liverpool and Manchester, opened in 1830, was one of the first to rely also entirely upon steam traction, and one whereon passenger traffic was

reckoned as important as, if not more important than, goods. Accommodation was provided for first-, second- and third-class passengers, and our picture illustrating one of the earliest first-class carriages on the line clearly shows how the earliest designs were based upon the traditional style of a stage coach. The experienced coach builders were called upon to provide railway carriages, and one can readily imagine the 'Traveller' carriage as three stage-coach bodies in one. The principal difference between road and rail coaches is that in the latter no accommodation was provided for outside passengers – somewhat naturally, in view of the smoke and sparks emitted by the early locomotives; but tradition was continued in that outside seats were provided for the guard, and luggage was loaded on to the roof. This latter practice was combined for many years on railways; but it became recognized as a source of considerable danger, in that sparks from the engines could lodge among the various packages and cause fires. The earliest railways had no station platforms as we know them today and passengers had to clamber up from ground level by the rather primitive steps. As crinolines were still in vogue at the time of the earliest railways, climbing up must have been something of a feat for the ladies.

4 **Third-class carriage;** Liverpool and Manchester Railway.
In the earliest days of railways there was little encouragement for third-class passengers to travel – rather the reverse. Accommodation was provided in open trucks, but to those orders of society who had been accustomed to walk if they wished to travel anywhere, a ride in an open third-class carriage, even in the depths of winter, was no great hardship. The only change from braving the elements was that one had to brave the smoke and exhaust fumes from the locomotives. The amenities for second-class passengers lay midway between those of the 'firsts' and the 'thirds'. The carriages were open at the sides, but had a canopy over the top to keep out some of the weather. As the travelling habit began to grow, and many people who had never travelled in their lives began to venture on to the railways, the cry arose for better third-class carriages. One hears of coaches having holes drilled in the floors to let the water out, and on the other hand of a riotous company flinging empty bottles at men working on the line. Many a cherished top hat was lost when gusts of wind caused by the speed of the train caught its owner unprepared; though to be sure there was a certain clergyman who said he always travelled third class on the railway because there was not a fourth class! There were some seats in the open trucks; but more often than not there were far more passengers than seats and the earliest third-class trains bore a striking resemblance in the way passengers were huddled together to present-day rush-hour traffic on the London Underground.

5 **First-class carriage;** North Union Railway.
As railway travelling became more popular the amenities of travel gradually increased and the particular illustration shows an interesting development of the stage-coach type of first-class carriage. But before referring more particularly, a word is necessary about the railway itself. The system of railways extending from London up the western side of England owes a great deal to the far-sightedness and enterprise of the central partner – the Grand Junction, which linked the London and Birmingham with the Liverpool and Manchester, at a point about midway between the two last-mentioned cities. But the management of the Grand Junction had visions of an enterprise of much greater extent, one which eventually took the metals of its partners as far

north as Aberdeen. The Lancaster and Preston Junction was another link in the chain, and to connect the latter with the Grand Junction proper the North Union Railway was projected from Preston, through Wigan to Newton. This North Union had one coupé compartment at the end, with observation windows, while beneath the windows the body was chariot-shaped. There was a close compartment for luggage, the buffers were stuffed with horse hair, and a notable amenity is to be seen in the oil lamps. Lighting was at one time considered quite unnecessary. A complaint was once made to Brunel about the darkness of Box Tunnel. He replied that the tunnel was no darker than the rest of the line was at night!

6 **Tri-composite four-wheeler of Monmouthshire Railway design;** Great Western Railway.

This carriage, primitive though it looks, represented a great advance upon early railway standards. In 1844 W. E. Gladstone was President of the Board of Trade, and he piloted through Parliament a Bill that required all railways to provide covered-in carriages for third-class passengers to serve all stations, at a standard fare of one penny per mile. Some of the less progressive railways took unkindly to this legislation and provided nothing more than forbidding closed-in boxes for third-class passengers, and ran the so-called 'Parliamentary' trains at night. For many years the term Parliamentary, or Parley as they were more often called among railwaymen, was applied to any stop-at-all-stations slow train. The tri-composite coach shown in our picture reveals the lingerings of stage-coach design styles in the windows of the first- and second-class compartments, while in the 'thirds' windows were provided only in the doors, as though to keep passengers of more lowly orders concealed out of sight. This coach was designed in 1851 for the Monmouthshire Railway, a line later absorbed by the Great Western Railway. The builder was J. Wright, a noted coach manufacturer of the period. The coach is shown in our picture in the traditional chocolate and cream of the G.W.R., which dates from the very early days of that railway.

7 **Stirling 7 ft. 7 in. 2-2-2 Single;** Great Northern Railway.

Patrick Stirling, Locomotive Superintendent of the G.N.R. from 1866 to 1895, will always be remembered by his beautiful bogie 8 ft. single express locomotives, with outside cylinders. But these engines were in a class apart, in that they were the only ones he built having outside cylinders. All the rest, goods engines, suburban tanks, mixed traffic and express passenger alike, had inside cylinders, and an extremely neat exterior, with all the machinery discreetly hidden. The very handsome engine illustrated was one of a class introduced in 1886 for working turn and turn about with the bogie 8-footers on the fastest express duties. They were very successful engines, and ran freely at really high speeds. The Great Northern passenger services of those days were among the fastest anywhere in the world. In the great railway race of 1895 one of this class, No. 874, took the 8 p.m. Aberdeen express from Kings Cross to Grantham $105\frac{1}{2}$ miles in $112\frac{3}{4}$ min. with a load that would be considered heavy for so fast a run – 190 tons. The 27 miles from Hitchin to Huntingdon were covered in $24\frac{1}{2}$ min., and the maximum speed was just short of 80 m.p.h. Unfortunately, these engines were introduced at a time when train loads were very much on the increase, and by the early years of the twentieth century they were outclassed. Of the 21 engines built to this design, the majority had a life of less than 20 years, which was very short for a well-designed and efficient locomotive of that period.

8 **Four-wheeled brake-third carriage;** Great Northern Railway.
The Great Northern had, both for its locomotives and its passenger stock, one of the most pleasing liveries to be seen anywhere. Behind the light-green engines, always so immaculately turned out, there ran trains of coaches in which the teak of their construction was given no other finish than varnish. But it was done so well that the effect was superb. The Great Northern, like its age-old rival on the West Coast route from Euston, was a convinced user of non-bogie coaches, even for the fastest main-line expresses, and the Aberdeen 'racer' of 1895, although making average speeds in excess of 60 m.p.h. was composed entirely of 6-wheeled stock. The coach illustrated is one used in a set of close-coupled London suburban vehicles, as will be appreciated from the truncated buffer at the right-hand end in the picture. If coupling and uncoupling had to be done regularly, as in the case of some main-line formations, these short buffers would have been most inconvenient; but the suburban trains were kept in close-coupled sets, and in a long train there was some saving in overall length. The Great Northern suburban coaches, although cramped by modern standards, were considerably less spartan than some of their neighbours, and the partitions between compartments were taken up to the roof. The roofs themselves, when newly turned out of the shops, were white. This may have seemed a most impractical colour, but there was no intention of trying to keep them so. The white lead paint used was found to be excellent in its lasting qualities, and it soon 'weathered' to a pleasing grey, as shown in this picture.

9 **Coniston branch 2-2-2 tank engine;** Furness Railway.
The Furness Railway, although isolated by geography from the major arteries of through railway traffic in Great Britain, came to have a notably high tradition in engineering matters. Its association with the iron and steel industry in its own neighbourhood, and with the great works of Messrs. Vickers, at Barrow-in-Furness, naturally brought its men into contact with the latest developments in heavy engineering production, and the outcome was a particularly fine range of steam locomotives for all classes of duty, albeit on a scale limited by the size and traffic of the railway. The dainty little 2-2-2 tank engine illustrated belongs nevertheless to an earlier period, when the position of the Furness Railway was being consolidated. It was built by Sharp Stewart and Co. Ltd., in 1866, specially for working on the picturesque branch line from Foxfield to Coniston. Although this line, in climbing into the mountains overlooking Coniston Lake, is heavily graded, the traffic was light in early days and a locomotive with cylinders no larger than 15 in. diameter by 18 in. stroke; driving wheels of 5 ft. 6 in. diameter, and a boiler pressure of 120 lb. per sq. in. was quite adequate. The water supply was carried in a well tank – invisible in the picture – having a capacity of 500 gallons. This illustration shows admirably the beautiful locomotive livery of the Furness Railway – a very appropriate iron-ore red – and characteristic of the colour of the soil in many parts of the country through which the railway ran.

10 **Sir James Ramsden's Inspection Car;** Furness Railway.
The higher management of the Furness Railway was, so far as can be traced, unique in Great Britain, in that the directors gave their services entirely free, regarding this work as a social service to the districts served by the railway. The supreme command again was unusual in being vested in a Managing Director, in the person of Sir James Ramsden – a very prominent figure in Barrow. In 1865 Wright Brothers built the picturesque

little coach illustrated specially for Sir James to use during inspections of the line. There were two compartments inside; but one was made narrow so that one could see both fore and aft from the other. The picture shows the open platform at the back, which was used for outside observation, if necessary. This vehicle was in constant use by Sir James Ramsden for upwards of thirty years, indeed up to the time of his retirement. The colour of the vehicle, as shown in the illustration, is that of the first carriages of the Furness Railway, a rich varnished wood closely matching that of the locomotives; but in later years, as shown in subsequent pictures in this book, a beautiful two-colour scheme of Royal blue and white was adopted. It is pleasant to recall that the management of the Furness Railway was always historically minded, and this inspection vehicle was included among a series of picture postcards issued in years before World War I; this series also included a picture of the Duke of Devonshire's private carriage – another quaint old four-wheeler dating from the 1850s.

11 **Suburban Tank Engine;** London, Chatham and Dover type.
The London, Chatham and Dover Railway, in the complexity of its lines in the London suburban area, was one of the most difficult of systems to manage, and reference was made in the *Pocket Encyclopaedia of British Steam Locomotives* to the 0-4-2 tank engines of the 'Scotchmen' series introduced by William Martley. These were splendid little machines, and although introduced as long ago as 1866 they were still hard at work in 1898, when the company was brought into association with its old rival, the South Eastern Railway, under a Managing Committee, and locomotives of both companies thenceforth bore the initials S.E.&C.R. Legally and financially there was never such a concern as the 'South Eastern and Chatham Railway', and close scrutiny of the heraldic device carried on the express locomotives revealed the reference to the Managing Committee. But under the new working arrangement all the locomotives of both companies were decked in a very bright and gay livery of fresh green, plentifully ornamented with polished brass, and much attractive lining. The 'Scotchmen' 0-4-2 tank engines had by that time been reboilered and, as our picture shows, acquired a more modern look than in their original form of 1866. In S.E.&C.R. days, nevertheless, they were among the smartest and prettiest little tank engines working in and around London.

12 **The 'Single' No. 123;** Caledonian Railway.
This celebrated engine, a completely isolated specimen built by Neilson & Co. and exhibited at the Edinburgh Exhibition of 1886, has in 80 years achieved a fame that would have astonished her builders had they lived to witness it. Dugald Drummond was building powerful new 4-4-0 locomotives for the heavily graded routes of the Caledonian Railway; and it was remarkable in the first place that they should have ordered also a single-wheeler, with the same boiler and machinery. No. 123 was greatly admired at the Edinburgh Exhibition, but two years later, in 1888, it was shown that she was no mere ornament. In the Race to the North she had the task of hauling the racing train from Carlisle to Edinburgh, and her fastest journey gave an average speed of 60 m.p.h., even though the 1,014 ft. altitude of Beattock summit had to be surmounted and a second heavy climb from Carstairs to Cobbinshaw also made. In later years No. 123 was set aside by the Caledonian Railway to haul the Directors' Inspection Saloon; but after the grouping of the railways in 1923, and the inclusion of the Caledonian in the

L.M.S. system, this duty was no longer required, and No. 123, by that time re-numbered 14010, returned to ordinary passenger service, chiefly on local trains between Perth and Dundee. As such she became the last single-wheeler in Great Britain to remain in revenue earning service. After her eventual withdrawal she was saved from the scrapheap and restored to the Caledonian livery for preservation. In recent years she has been further re-novated to full working order, and has done much excellent working in the haulage of enthusiasts' special trains in many parts of the country. As preserved now she has the later type of small Caledonian boiler, with plain dome, and Ramsbottom safety valves over the fire-box. She is also in the bright blue livery, familiar to travellers in Scotland in the twentieth century. Our picture shows her in original condition, as she ran in the Race of 1888; the safety valves were then on the dome, in the traditional Drum-mond style, and the livery was the very distinguished Prussian blue.

13 **Rebuilt Cudworth 2-4-0 loco-motive;** South Eastern Railway.
The trunk route from London to Dover had a most curious and complicated origin. One might have imagined that in the projecting of railway communica-tion over a route that had connections across the English Channel to all parts of Europe, and by the overland route to India and the Far East, would have in-volved nothing more nor less than a direct line. Instead such were the initial pecuniary difficulties that use was made of the Brighton railway as far as Redhill, and there the line to Dover swept round sharply at right angles, and then ran almost dead straight for Ashford, before turning towards Folkestone. Cudworth built some good engines for the line, but other circumstances precluded any chance of really fast running. The engine shown in our picture is one of his numerous 2-4-0 passenger class, but as rebuilt by James Stirling. This was an interesting example of a rebuild in which the second version was really a prettier machine than the original. The colours are those in vogue in the latter part of the Victorian era, when these engines were used on branch-line passenger trains, and on lighter express trains. No fewer than 124 of them were originally built, between 1857 and 1875, and at the latter date they formed roughly half the entire locomotive stock of the South Eastern Railway. In their rebuilt form as illustrated quite a number of them survived after 1899 to bear the colours of the South Eastern and Chatham Managing Committee.

14 **Midland and Great Northern Joint Railway;** 2-4-0 passenger engine.
A glance at the picture of this pretty little engine immediately suggests a strong connection with Alexander Allan in the form of the front-end framing and the spacing of the wheels. It certainly is an Allan engine, but the connection with the designer, so far as the 'M.&G.N.' was concerned, was exceedingly indirect. The Midland and Great Northern Joint Railway was a somewhat 'indirect' affair itself, and a note on its origins will help to explain how it came to possess two Allan engines. Despite the weight of Great Eastern influence in East Anglia, one or two local railways in North Norfolk tried to pursue independent careers, such as the Yarmouth and North Norfolk, and the Lynn and Fakenham. With some lines west of Kings Lynn, these fragments were at first gathered together under the title of the Eastern and Mid-lands Railway, in 1883, and then the whole concern came under the joint ownership of the Midland and the Great Northern Railways. Between them, the two large companies worked the joint line up into a very creditable, if not very pro-fitable, business, and in the summer they handled a very heavy Saturday holiday

traffic from the Midlands to East Anglia. But in days before the joint ownership the 'Eastern and Midlands' was constantly in financial difficulties, and they were compelled to buy what locomotives they could pick up cheaply – second, third or even fourth hand. Naturally a somewhat heterogeneous collection assembled in East Anglia, and the two Allan 2-4-0s were bought from the London and North Western Railway, in 1883. They had originally been allocated to the Lancaster and Carlisle section, and one of the two was employed as a slow-train engine on the Ingleton branch, working between that town and Tebay. The 'M.&G.N.' made it look very smart in their mustard yellow livery, and as illustrated it bore the initials in full on the tender. In later days the initials were just 'M.&G.N.'

15 **London Suburban Carriage;** Midland Railway.

In pre-grouping days the Midland Railway had one of the most distinctive liveries of any company, with engines and carriages alike in a rich shade of crimson lake. In more recent years this colour, or a modern synthetic version of it, became much more familiar to the travelling public as the livery of the L.M.S., and it has now been adopted as standard for British Railways. The little four-wheeler illustrated may seem a rather primitive thing, but in late Victorian days the Midland, by abolishing second-class carriages into thirds, provided much better accommodation for the third-class passenger than was to be found on most other lines. The seats were cushioned, and if the head-rests were plain boards at least the partitions extended up to the ceilings. The carriage illustrated was used on the service into the heart of the City of London, over the so-called 'widened lines' of the Metropolitan Railway from Kings Cross to Moorgate. Over this section of the Inner Circle there were then, as now, four tracks, and the steam-hauled trains of the Midland and of the Great Northern descended to the level of the Underground by steeply-graded and sharply-curved tunnels from their own lines. While the Great Northern tunnels came to the surface adjacent to Kings Cross station, the Midland lines surfaced about half-way between St. Pancras and Kentish Town.

16 **Second-Class Suburban Carriage;** Great Eastern Railway.

The steam-hauled suburban service of the Great Eastern, worked from its terminal stations at Liverpool Street and Fenchurch Street, was one of the phenomena of the railway network of London. Most of the trains were made up of entirely four-wheeled coaches, close-coupled as can be inferred by the design of the buffers shown in our illustration, and including first-, second- and third-class carriages. The 'firsts' were quite luxurious in their seating, though they rode rather 'hard'. The 'seconds' were much more cramped, and although having cushioned seats were straight-backed, and gave little room for the knees. The 'thirds' sat on bare boards, and the partitions extended only to shoulder-height. A third-class carriage was thus virtually open, and one could easily climb over the partition from one section to another. But although the accommodation was spartan for the majority of travellers, the service was very smartly run. There were literally swarms of trains, and to see them follow each other out of Liverpool Street in the evening rush-hour was an object lesson as to what could be done when efficient steam locomotives were backed by a superb operating organization. Stopping times at intermediate stations were reckoned in seconds rather than minutes, and to enable passengers of the three classes to recognize their compartments quickly the doors were at one time painted in bright distinctive colours. This led to the nickname 'Jazz Trains', but while the coloured doors are now long forgotten by the public the Liverpool Street suburban service has ever since been known to railwaymen as 'the jazz', even now that it is changed out of all recognition, and worked by electric multiple unit trains.

17 **Local Train Carriage;** Great Western Railway.
In contrast to the majority of railways that worked into London the G.W.R. never developed an intensive suburban service of its own. This was partly due to geography, in that during the nineteenth century the busiest and most populous suburbs grew up in the north-eastern and in the south of London, and partly due to one of those dramatic pieces of inter-railway warfare that enlivened the development of the transport network of this country in mid-Victorian times. The original line of the underground Metropolitan Railway ran from Farringdon Street to a junction with the Great Western, adjoining Paddington station, and it was originally laid mixed gauge. The passenger service was in fact provided in broad gauge carriages by the Great Western. But a sharp disagreement over the frequency of service led to the withdrawal of Great Western stock, and for a time this potentially lucrative traffic was lost. The carriage illustrated is typical of those used on the numerous country branch services of the G.W.R., on which the tempo of life was the very opposite of the rush and bustle of London suburban trains. Station stops were leisurely, during which the driver, fireman and guard greeted their friends among the local railwaymen and residents, and when a train would be held waiting if a regular passenger, however humble his or her status, was late in arriving at the station. The mileage worked daily by the coaching stock was in keeping with the spacious air of the general proceedings and the coach illustrated was one of a small set allocated to the 5 p.m. train from Bala to Ruabon. Apparently it had little other duty, because that train was duly painted on the solebars.

18 **Four-wheeled coach;** North London Railway.
This busy and prosperous little railway was in many ways a smaller counterpart of the Great Eastern, in the character and operation of its passenger traffic. Its terminal station, at Broad Street, in the City of London, was adjacent to the great Liverpool Street terminus of the G.E.R., and its coaching stock was similar, both in colour and in the agility with which vast numbers of passengers were packed into incredibly small compartments. From Dalston Junction its lines fanned out into three directions, and the centre one of these climbed over the 'northern heights' to serve Hampstead. The days when those cramped little four-wheeled coaches disgorged city workers in their hundreds, and even quite humble clerks would be wearing tall hats and morning coats, take some imagining today. But in addition to the services of its own the North London had running powers over the Great Northern Railway, which was reached at Finsbury Park through a connection by Canonbury Tunnel. The little North London 4-4-0 tank engines, and their long trains of close-coupled four-wheeled coaches, used to work out to Potters Bar, on the main line, and up the steep gradients of the High Barnet branch. The further ramifications of the North London are referred to under reference 26, wherein its coat of arms is described.

19 **Webb eight-wheeled radial coach;** London and North Western Railway.
In the nineteenth century there was considerable reluctance among British railway managements to adopt longer

passenger vehicles. Most main-line express trains were composed of six-wheeled coaches, and not infrequently included some four-wheelers. It is true that the clearances existing in some sidings and platforms precluded the use of longer vehicles, but in many ways the introduction of bogie vehicles had been retarded by the excellence of British permanent way. In America, where bogie vehicles were in regular service, the standards of track maintenance were not so high, and the greater flexibility of the bogie coach provided some compensation against irregularities in the line and level of the track. The introduction of bogie coaches were resisted nowhere more strongly than on the London and North Western; but the advantage of longer coaches was equally realized, and F. W. Webb, the celebrated Chief Mechanical Engineer, designed an eight-wheeled coach in which flexibility in the wheelbase was provided by making two of the axles capable of radial movement to suit the curves of the line. On a route so relatively free from sharp curves these coaches with radial axles were quite successful, and provided a very smooth ride. The 'racing' train of 1888 which ran at unprecedented speeds between Euston and Edinburgh was composed of four of these vehicles, though the smooth riding was partly due to the care taken to see that all the coaches were tightly coupled at the ends with the spring buffers slightly compressed together.

20 **T. G. Clayton's twelve-wheeled 'brake-third'**; Midland Railway.
The opening of the Settle and Carlisle line in 1876 and the inauguration of through express services to Glasgow and Edinburgh marked a very important stage in the development of the Midland Railway. For the new trains Clayton built some twelve-wheeled carriages that for comfort and smooth riding were marvels for that period. They had high clerestory roofs, but these were not entirely a success, and condensation from the small windows in the clerestory led to the dripping of moisture on passengers. In the next batch of main-line coaches the clerestory roof was abandoned, from 1877 onwards, and our picture shows a typical Midland main-line carriage of the period between then and about 1900. Its great length will be noted, and no less the generous width of compartment inside, evident from the wide spacing of the windows. The wheels had wooden centres, and this resulted in very quiet riding. The Midland was a pioneer in providing very comfortable carriages for third-class passengers, and for the period these could certainly be considered as the finest 'ordinary' carriages running in Great Britain. So far as the Scotch services were concerned, the company was breaking in upon the established business of the London and North Western and Great Northern Railways, neither of which was over-generous in its accommodation at that time. Passengers had to be tempted away, by the magnificence of the Midland trains.

21 **Broad-gauge composite carriage;** Great Western Railway.
The era of the broad gauge on the Great Western Railway will always remain one of the greatest epics, romances, and tragedies of British railway history. The company's first Chief Engineer, the great Isambard Kingdom Brunel, felt that the rail gauge of the old colliery tramways in the north of England, which George Stephenson was perpetuating in the passenger-carrying railways he was constructing, imposed far too great a limitation on future development; and not without a great deal of opposition he persuaded the Great Western Board to sanction his use of the seven-foot gauge, as against the northern standard of 4 ft. 8½ in. There is no doubt he imagined that once a magnificent line like the original

Great Western Railway from London to Bristol was in operation, its advantages would be so obvious that everyone else would change to the broad gauge. And when the Great Western commenced working it would certainly not have been too late to do so. Unfortunately for Brunel he remained the 'odd man out'; but between the incorporation of the Great Western Railway by Act of Parliament in 1835, and the final conversion of the gauge in 1892, the 'broad gauge' built up its remarkable aura of romance and epic struggle. One of the claims strongly put forward in its favour by Brunel was the spaciousness of the carriages, and our picture shows one of these exceptional vehicles. The third-class compartments seated no fewer than 9-aside. As the time for final conversion drew near, many coaches used on the broad-gauge lines were built with narrow bodies, so that when the time of conversion came these bodies could be transferred, with little trouble, from broad gauge to narrow-gauge frames; but our picture shows one of the maximum width broad-gauge carriages. The tragedy of the broad gauge was two-fold: that the opportunity was lost of a more spacious railway system that would have been a godsend in dealing with the tremendous problems of city commuter traffic, and that the personal tragedy for Brunel greatly shortened his brilliant life.

22 **Boat Train six-wheeler;** South Eastern Railway.

Coaching stock was not the strongest feature of the railways running south-eastwards from London. The South Eastern itself had an extraordinarily heterogeneous collection of rolling stock of all shapes and sizes, so much so that a wit once described their trains as looking like a moving castellated caravan – no two adjacent coaches being of the same height. Furthermore, the need for economy in expenditure led to these coaches falling into a somewhat decrepit condition, and the old two-tone colour scheme of pink upper panels and brown bodies could look woebegone in the extreme. But if the passengers in local trains, and also in the mid-week 'Cheap fasts' to the seaside, had to put up with vehicles that became nicknamed 'dog-boxes', there was nothing parsimonious about the stock provided for the Continental boat trains, even before the introduction of bogie coaches. Our picture shows a very smart carriage that was typical of the boat trains in late Victorian times. In this respect the trains of the South Eastern and of its rival the London Chatham and Dover were an excellent advertisement for Great Britain. They were vastly superior to the carriages used at that time in France and Belgium, which were not only dingy in outward appearance, both in their basic colour and the state of their upkeep, but also in their interior appointments and general comfort.

23 **Coat of Arms;** London and North Western Railway.

Some of the most interesting and colourful points of detail connected with the old railways of Britain were centred upon their 'Coats of Arms'. In calling them coats of arms, however, it must be admitted that in many cases the devices displayed on locomotives and carriages had no heraldic justification, and were not railway counterparts of the crest and coat of arms, in the heraldry of old English families. The crest of the London and North Western Railway was a case in point. It is true that this great joint-stock corporation claimed to be the oldest established firm in the railway business, and that its sphere of activity extended far beyond the territory suggested by its name. But its crest had as its centrepiece Britannia herself, and the British lion. It was surrounded by a profusion of ornamental scrolls, but with nothing in the way of a motto, or other explanation. Although an earlier version of this device had been used for various purposes, its first use as an item of decoration for locomotives did not occur till the 1880s, when it was put on to the Webb 18-inch express goods 0-6-0 engines. For a time these engines were known as the 'Crested Goods'; but before long the enginemen had found a much more homely nickname which has lasted ever since. They called the engines the 'Cauliflowers', and one had to agree that seen at a little distance, when the detail became a little blurred, that 'crest' could look uncommonly like a cauliflower! Although the crest was subsequently applied to all express passenger engines, the 18-inch 'Crested Goods' were always known as the 'Cauliflowers'.

24 **Coat of Arms;** Midland Railway.
There were many points of strong contrast between the London and North Western and the Midland Railways, and in the coat of arms adopted in the early years of the twentieth century the Midland had a device that was not only very beautiful in itself but which had a strong historical significance. In its origins no railway was more aptly named. It was born out of an amalgamation between the Midland Counties Railway, the Birmingham and Derby, and the North Midland. It had not extended north of Leeds nor south of Rugby. When its new coat of arms was designed it had extended enormously: the main line ran from London to Carlisle, and south-westwards to Bath and Bristol; while its through carriages penetrated to Bournemouth and Torquay, to Glasgow and Edinburgh, and in the high season to Inverness. Nevertheless, in its heraldic device the Midland remained faithful to its origin. Its crest was the Wyvern of Mercia, and the shield incorporated those of six of the largest centres of activity in the original orbit of the company: Birmingham, with the chains, screws and other insignia of manufactories; Derby; Bristol, with its association with the Merchant Venturers; Leicester, Lincoln, and Leeds. The inclusion of Lincoln might perhaps be questioned, but the cross-country line from Derby through Nottingham and Newark was an important feature of Midland strategy to cut across and deeply into the territory of the rival Great Northern Railway. As such the arms of the city of Lincoln had to occupy a centrepiece on the shield as prominent as that of Derby, which latter place always remained the headquarters of the Midland, even after the London extension had been completed.

25 **Coat of Arms;** Lancashire and Yorkshire Railway.
This beautiful device, which was carried on engines and carriages alike, was one of the simplest of railway emblems for the travelling public to understand. For it included the red and white roses of the Royal Houses of Lancaster and York, surmounting the shields of those two ancient cities. Curiously enough, however, the Lancashire and Yorkshire Railway did not reach either Lancaster or York on its own tracks. Its engines and trains worked into York over the metals of the North Eastern Railway, but so far as Lancaster was concerned its traffic associations extended to no more than the through services worked from Liverpool and Manchester to Scotland. These were hauled through Lancaster by London and North Western locomotives. The Lancashire and Yorkshire Railway was a line of the teeming industrial regions clustered around what could be termed the Liverpool-Manchester-Leeds 'axis'. The old Manchester and Leeds Railway was indeed one of its major constituents, and from that origin branches and subsidiary main lines penetrated into the hilly, highly industrialized country on both sides of the Pennines. Although it

did not reach Lancaster itself and the fringes of the Lake District, nor the wide-open spaces of the North and East Riding, as a thoroughgoing industrial concern no railway was more aptly named than the Lancashire and Yorkshire.

26 **Coat of Arms;** North London Railway.
The group of coats of arms illustrated under references 23 to 26 all relate to concerns that were eventually included in the London Midland and Scottish Railway. Two were great trunk lines that extended from London to Carlisle, usually in strong competition with each other. The third, although a local enterprise, became one of great influence and prestige. Nevertheless, to judge by its coat of arms, in the beauty of its design and colouring, one could well imagine the North London could hold its own with the best! And among the four quarters of its shield will be noticed with some surprise that of Birmingham. How could this purely local London railway claim any connection with Birmingham? This line was originally known as 'The East and West India Docks and Birmingham Junction Railway'. From its inception, however, it was closely associated with the London and North Western, and one of the lines radiating from Dalston Junction ran almost due west to join the North Western at Chalk Farm, at the eastern end of Primrose Hill Tunnel. It was not until the twentieth century that this connection was used for anything more than purely local service. Then the interesting 'City to City' express service was introduced between Birmingham and Broad Street, thus after many years fulfilling the ambitions of the North London in having Birmingham on its coat of arms. The quarterings were as follows: top left, the shield of the East India Dock Company; top right, Birmingham; bottom left, the City of London; and bottom right, the entrance gateway to the West India Import Dock.

27 **The** *Greater Britain* **engine of 1891;** London and North Western Railway.
For some years prior to the building of this remarkable engine F. W. Webb, Chief Mechanical Engineer of the L.& N.W.R., had been using three-cylinder compound locomotives for the heaviest express passenger work. All these engines were six-wheelers, with two high-pressure cylinders outside the frames and a single low-pressure cylinder inside. These drove on to the rear and leading pairs of driving wheels respectively, and as can be seen in the illustration, the two pairs of driving wheels were not coupled. This sometimes led to differential slipping, and some difficulty in starting a heavy train. But in developing the three-cylinder compound system from the 'Teutonic' class of 1889 Webb designed a very much larger boiler, making it longer rather than increasing the diameter, so as to avoid too great a concentration of dead weight. To avoid the disadvantage of very long flue tubes he used an intermediate combustion chamber, so that the exhaust gases from the firebox passed through one set of tubes; then through the combustion chamber, and then through a further set of tubes before reaching the smokebox. To accommodate the extra length of boiler a pair of trailing wheels was provided under the firebox, and as thus built the *Greater Britain* was one of the longest engines yet to appear in this country. Its unusual livery is referred to later, under reference 29, relating to the *Queen Empress*.

28 **West Coast Joint Stock coach.**
Up to the time of the grouping of the railways in 1923 the express services between London and the Scottish cities were operated by a number of independent railways working in partnership.

Thus, from Kings Cross one travelled over the tracks, successively, of the Great Northern, the North Eastern, and of the North British Railway to reach Edinburgh, while from Euston it was the London and North Western and the Caledonian that were in partnership in providing services from London to both Edinburgh and Glasgow. Similarly, on the Midland route from St. Pancras, that railway was associated with both the North British and the Glasgow and South Western, in Scotland. On all these routes 'joint' rolling stock, reserved specially for the regular Anglo-Scottish expresses, was provided. The West Coast vehicles, working from Euston, carried the initials 'W.C.J.S.', and a special crest, illustrated under reference 55. At the time of their introduction it was a remarkable coincidence that those initials were also those of the general managers of the London and North Western and Caledonian Railways, namely William Cawkwell and James Smithells. The carriages of the West Coast Joint Stock were always built to London and North Western designs, at Wolverton works, and in general followed standard North Western practice, of which the coach illustrated was a typical example.

29 **The Diamond Jubilee celebration engines;** London and North Western Railway.
In the year 1891, when Webb's large 2-2-2-2 compound express locomotives were introduced, the growth of the British Empire was an increasing source of national pride and satisfaction. In the year 1877 Queen Victoria had assumed the title of Empress of India, and the name *Greater Britain* applied to the first of the new engines was a natural expression of popular sentiment at the time. For two years it remained an isolated engine, while extensive trials were in progress. It ran in the standard L.&N.W.R. colours, glossy black, with red, cream and light grey lining; but in 1893 a second engine was built, the *Queen Empress*, and again in the standard 'black' sent to the Chicago Exhibition. Eight more engines of the class were built in 1894. In the year of the Diamond Jubilee however, 1897, the engines *Greater Britain* and *Queen Empress* were specially painted in celebration of the event. *Greater Britain* was decked in scarlet, with the Royal Arms on one of the driving-wheel splashers and on the tender, while *Queen Empress* was painted in *white*! At the time it was thought that there were eventually to be three specially painted engines: one red; one white; and one blue. But actually the 'red, white and blue' were all incorporated on the *Greater Britain*, which had the smokebox and wheel centres blue, and white wheel rims. The *Queen Empress* carried an extraordinarily beautiful, but somewhat impracticable livery, of a soft creamy white, with lavender edging and thus symbolical of the elderly lady after whom the engine was named. Somewhat naturally the standard L.&N.W.R. livery was restored soon after the period of the Diamond Jubilee celebrations had passed.

30 **One of the first dining cars;** London and North Western Railway.
The reluctance of the North Western authorities to depart from six-wheeled coaches has been referred to earlier in connection with Webb's radial axles, reference 19; but having obtained such good riding from the West Coast Joint Stock used in the racing train of 1888, it is not a little surprising that when dining cars were first introduced, on the Liverpool and Manchester expresses from London in 1889, a reversion to six-wheelers should have been made. They were available only to first-class passengers, and seated no more than 14 passengers, with only one chair on either side of the gangway. They were run in pairs, connected to each other, but without any

connection to the rest of the train, so that once in the dining car one stayed there for the rest of the journey. The companion car contained the so-called 'dining and smoking saloon', which seated 8 passengers; also the kitchen, and what was described on the original drawing as the 'butler's pantry'. Our picture of one of these cars was prepared from a copy of the original drawing still preserved at Wolverton works, and this drawing helps to recreate something of the spacious atmosphere of the period, not only in the exquisite draughtsmanship, but in the use of 'Old English' lettering in the titles. Imagine a modern engineering drawing office having time for such adornment of its documents.

31 **Short-coupled 0-6-0 mineral engine;** North Eastern Railway.
In bringing under one management the locomotives of four such individual concerns as the York and North Midland, the Leeds Northern, the York, Newcastle and Berwick and the Stockton and Darlington, the responsible engineers had an almost insuperable task when it came to the first attempts at standardization. Edward Fletcher never really seriously attempted it; but by his own skill and kindly nature he brought a high degree of efficiency and reliability to this exceeding diverse stud of locomotives as well as imparting to them an exceedingly picturesque appearance. Our picture shows a coal engine of 1866 as 'modernized' by Mr. Fletcher. It is astonishing to recall that engines engaged in heavy mineral traffic, between the mining areas and the ports from which coal was exported, should have had such a highly decorative finish. Not only so, but that they were kept spotlessly clean. Technical features of these engines were the very long boilers, which were well suited to the job of working the mineral trains; the picturesque outside frames, and outside cranks, and the double safety valves, so frequently to be seen on many nineteenth-century locomotives. One set, of the Salter-type spring-balance type, was on the dome, and the other was contained in the brass column over the firebox. These engines did excellent work and many survived into the twentieth century.

32 **Kirtley 2-4-0 No. 158A;** Midland Railway.
Matthew Kirtley, Locomotive Superintendent of the Midland Railway from 1844 to 1873, was one of the most successful of mid-Victorian engine designers. He was no scientist, or man of theory; but a practical engineer who had risen from the ranks, and knew precisely what was needed to work a heavy traffic with reliability, and a remarkable degree of efficiency. In 1866 he built the '156' class of 2-4-0s at Derby, and in them he achieved one of his greatest successes. The original engines were good enough, but it was their massive construction that enabled them to be twice rebuilt, and their cylinders enlarged from the original 16½ in. by 22 in. up to 18 in. by 24 in. Our picture shows the third engine of the class, No. 158, as numbered on the duplicate list – 158A, and as such she still exists today, carefully preserved, and of the ripe old age of 100 years. But much happened to her since she was renumbered No. 2 of the Midland Railway, in 1907. Fifteen years later she was still going strong and she became No. 2 of the L.M.S.R. – still handsomely painted in Derby red. Then she became 20002, and served all through World War II, painted plain black, and still in active service in 1945. She was taken out of traffic in 1948, after 82 years' service, and then most beautifully restored to her condition of the 1900–1907 period, and preserved. In this form she is a blend of the Kirtley and Johnson styles of engine designing: Kirtley frames and machinery, and a Johnson boiler.

33 **Mixed traffic 2-4-0 engine of 1877;** Caledonian Railway.
Until the appointment of Dugald Drummond as Locomotive Superintendent, in 1882, all Caledonian engines, passenger and goods alike, had outside cylinders. They had also the characteristic double framing at the front end, whereby the cylinders were snugly and massively ensconced; stove-pipe chimneys were the rule, and the driving-wheel splashers were slotted like the paddle-box of most packet steamers of the age. Under the superintendence of Benjamin Conner 2-2-2 singles with 8 ft. driving wheels had been built for the express traffic and when the loads became too great for single-wheelers Conner built 2-4-0s, with 7 ft. 2 in. wheels. The engine shown in our picture belongs to the intermediate class, with 6 ft. 2 in. coupled wheels, designed for stopping-train duties and branch-line work. They were excellent, sturdy little things, and survived on secondary work well into the twentieth century. A few of them were rebuilt by Dugald Drummond with larger boilers, as a stop-gap main-line passenger class pending the construction of his own very successful 4-4-0 engines. But many of the Conner engines, like No. 52 illustrated, remained unaltered. Some of them could be seen at Carlisle in the early 1900s, and although then relegated to the lightest of stopping trains they were still immaculately turned out, and as perfect little period pieces they stood out, among the very large 4-4-2 and 4-6-0 engines that were then being introduced on several of the railways running into Carlisle.

34 **'River' class 2-4-0** *Teign*; Great Western Railway.
These beautiful little engines, which in the form illustrated date from 1895, could be described as engines with a dual identity. There were eight of them in all, with numbers running from 69 to 76, and they originated in their first condition in 1872. At that time the broad gauge was still in full operation in the West of England, but the Great Western was also operating a considerable mileage on the standard gauge and these eight engines were built at Wolverhampton, as 2-2-2 singles for fast express working between Wolverhampton, Birmingham and Paddington. They did excellent work, but as with all engines the time came when they were no longer capable of working their original duties, and they were transferred to Swindon to help in the working of narrow-gauge expresses to Paddington. After the abolition of the broad gauge there was a general rearrangement of train services and they were no longer needed at Swindon. But their frames and machinery were still in excellent condition, and the eight engines were rebuilt as 2-4-0s in the very handsome style illustrated, and it was then that they received the added dignity of names – all after rivers in the West Country: *Avon, Dart, Dee, Exe, Isis, Stour, Teign*, and *Wye*. With their sandwich frames, and their profusion of brass and copperwork, they too were period pieces in the early 1900s; but they were sufficiently robust and serviceable engines for the last of them was to survive until 1918.

35 **East Coast Joint Stock sleeping-car.**
The 'joint stock' vehicle shown in this illustration dates from the early years of the twentieth century, and was one built by the North Eastern Railway, at York. Unlike the West Coast Joint Stock the East Coast was built variously by the Great Northern, North Eastern and North British Railways, and exhibited the design characteristics of the different works. Until the years 1905–6, high clerestory roofs had been used for large bogie vehicles, providing additional natural lighting and ventilation. But these were expensive to build – although very handsome in appearance (see reference

62) – and the North Eastern built sleeping-cars representing an attempt to get a simpler and cheaper form of construction. The panelled sides were quite flat, and the roofs elliptical. Like the traditional style of the East Coast Joint Stock, the finish was in varnished teak. The vehicle illustrated is of interest in that it was a 'composite' including both first- and third-class accommodation. Only the first-class passengers had proper sleeping-berths. There were only six single berths in the carriage, and two ordinary compartments for third-class passengers. It was not a very large vehicle, as East Coast Joint Stock went, measuring 56 ft. 5 in. over the end vestibule connections, but it represents a very interesting stage in the gradual evolution of accommodation for night travel between England and Scotland. Full berth accommodation for third-class passengers did not come till the late nineteen twenties.

36 **Llandudno Club Carriage;** London and North Western Railway.
In these days of private motor cars and the rapid development of very fast travel on trunk roads it is a little difficult to imagine the conditions in which the business tycoons in the first years of the present century travelled to and from their offices. Many magnates of the cotton industry whose activities were centred upon Manchester lived in the coastal resorts, such as Blackpool, Southport, and even as far away as towns on the North Wales coast. For them it was not enough to travel in first-class comfort, in fast non-stop trains; they must have club facilities on the journey, and in cooperation with the railway companies concerned some very interesting facilities were provided. Travelling clubs were formed, and special carriages provided to which only members were admitted. The accommodation was of the most luxurious kind, with each member having his own particular leather padded armchair, and the journey to and from the city could be a congenial and pleasant occasion. The Lancashire and Yorkshire Railway was one of the pioneers of this particular form of luxury service, and it became so popular that the so-called 'Club Trains' conveyed many more than one carriage for club members. The example chosen for illustration is one of the London and North Western Railway, operating between Manchester and Llandudno, and serving the resorts of Rhyl and Colwyn Bay en route.

37 **Morecambe Club Carriage;** Midland Railway.
The Midland was a railway of unbounding enterprise. Looking at a map of the system as it existed in the early years of the present century, one would hardly imagine it could emulate the practice of the Lancashire and Yorkshire, and London and North Western Railways in running attractive residential services from great centres of industry and commerce to seaside resorts. From Manchester it had no outlet to the Lancashire coast, or to North Wales, and while the North Eastern ran residential expresses from Leeds to Bridlington and Scarborough, the nearest resort to Leeds or Bradford on the Midland system was Morecambe. Sure enough, even though the route was not an easy one, and several intermediate points had to be catered for, the Midland developed a first-class residential service from Leeds and Bradford to Morecambe, and at the height of its enterprise put on a Club Carriage, running from Bradford. This handsome vehicle, reserved of course for club members only, made a daily journey of some 60 miles each way, with a journey time of about 1½ hours morning and evening, travelling over the Anglo-Scottish main line of the Midland Railway between Shipley and Settle Junction, and then through Giggleswick and the

moorland Clapham Junction to Lancaster, and so to journey's end on the shores of Morecambe Bay. Compared with the 35-mile run of the L.&Y.R. Manchester–Southport 'club' train, or even the fast 50-mile run of the Blackpool club train, it was a lengthy journey to make daily. But many people, quite apart from club members, travelled daily from Morecambe to both Bradford and Leeds.

38 **Ocean Liner Sleeping-Car;** London and South Western Railway.
In the early years of the present century liners of several nations, eastbound from the United States to Europe, called at Plymouth. By landing passengers there for British destinations considerable time could be saved over the more usual call at Southampton. Great importance was attached to this traffic by both the Great Western and the London and South Western Railways, and although there was a great rivalry between the two in respect of speed, there was agreement that the Great Western should take the mails, and the South Western the passengers. Special new train-sets were built, incorporating the most luxurious appointments considered desirable in the years 1900–5; but a further consideration was that the liners might arrive at any time during the 24 hours. While night running was not normally scheduled, a steamer could be delayed by fog or bad weather. Consequently the L.S.W.R. built some sleeping-cars specially for the ocean liner traffic, so that if a night run had to be made sleeping-berths were available. This service came to encounter a great tragedy in 1906, when one of these trains, for some quite unexplained reason, ran through Salisbury station at greatly excessive speed and was completely wrecked. In this disaster, coming suddenly in the dead of night, 24 out of the 43 ocean liner passengers travelling were killed. In later years the passenger traffic from the liners calling at Plymouth was taken over by the Great Western Railway.

39 **The Caledonian Railway coat of arms.**
The Caledonian Railway was one of the great institutions of Scottish life in years before the grouping of 1923. A study of the coat of arms, carried on engines and carriages alike, would suggest that it was a nationally-owned concern, because this insignia consisted of nothing more nor less than the Royal arms of Scotland, with the Royal mottoes included. Heraldically this device was without any justification, and probably without authority too! But in assuming this magnificent device the Caledonian was perpetuating a crucial point in its history. It was not by any means the first railway in Scotland, and its origin was the subject of acute controversy. The conception of a trunk line from Carlisle to Glasgow came from the Grand Junction Railway, and Scottish sentiment resented a project that had its origin in England! Nevertheless, many far-seeing Scots backed it wholeheartedly, while others were equally strong in their opposition. But to conceal the English influences in its origin the name Caledonian was chosen. Once launched the ambitions of the promoters knew no bounds, and one feels that the accent in the title was intended to be on *the*, and not necessarily on 'Caledonian'. In other words, it was to be *the* railway of Scotland – hence the adoption of the Royal arms. Other Scottish interests took a very different view, and the entire history of the railway right down to the time of its inclusion in the L.M.S.R. was of fierce rivalry with the other Scottish lines – particularly the Glasgow and South Western.

40 **The North British Railway coat of arms.**
In the nineteenth century, and indeed for some years afterwards, it was quite

usual to refer to Scotland as 'North Britain', and letters from England addressed to Scottish towns and villages had the letters 'N.B.' added, in addition to the normal address. The title 'North British Railway' could thus be construed as equally all-embracing as that of 'Caledonian'; and the two railways certainly had almost equal claims to be considered the premier line of Scotland. The North British, though of relatively limited extent, was of even older origin than the Caledonian, but had the distinction of being the first railway to cross the Anglo-Scottish border. Originally it extended only from Edinburgh to Berwick-upon-Tweed, and it is the arms of these two places that are embraced in its coat of arms, together with the thistle and the rose. But eventually the 'North British' came to include many other lines, including the much older Edinburgh and Glasgow Railway and the group of local lines around Edinburgh. Like the Caledonian the original name survived until the time of the grouping, though the country served by the 'N.B.R.' came to extend into the Western Highlands, and as far north as Fort Augustus. Yet its engines and carriages still carried the same coat of arms with the insignia only of Edinburgh and Berwick encircled within the garter.

41 **Highland Railway coat of arms.**
In every facet of its history and activities the Highland Railway was one of the most distinctive in the whole of Great Britain. The name itself dates from 1865, when the Inverness and Nairn, the Inverness and Aberdeen Junction, and the Inverness and Perth Junction Railways were amalgamated, and the line over the Grampian mountains was opened throughout. The company later came to include the various northern and western extensions from Inverness that eventually took the line to Wick and Thurso, and to the Kyle of Lochalsh. In the first place, however, the over-riding purpose of the railway promoters in Inverness was to establish direct connection with Perth, and it is this union by the line over the crest of the Grampians that is symbolized in the coat of arms. The Highland eagle is displayed, embracing in its outstretched wings the arms of the city of Perth, and the arms of the burgh of Inverness. Both are remarkable devices in themselves: that of Perth consists of the Holy Lamb, carrying the banner of St. Andrew, a device frequently used for inns having the more prosaic name of 'The Lamb and Flag'. The arms of the burgh of Inverness depicts our Lord upon the Cross, and thus both shields in the Highland Railway coat of arms have a deeply religious flavour. It was, however, not until relatively late in the history of the company that the full coat of arms was carried on locomotives, and then it was only used on the largest express passenger engines.

42 **The Glasgow and South Western Railway coat of arms.**
This railway, like the North British, retained for its entire lifetime the emblem of one of its earliest constituents. In the case of the G.&S.W.R. the emblem takes things right back to the very origin of railways in south-west Scotland. It was the emblem of the Glasgow, Paisley, Kilmarnock and Ayr Railway, which was incorporated as early as 1837. It was no less the existence of this railway that led to the acute controversy over the route of the proposed line from Carlisle to Glasgow. Purely Scottish interests argued that with a line already in existence as far south as Kilmarnock the new railway should be made to connect with it; and this argument was given an added force when the first surveys from the south, by Joseph Locke, favoured going via Dumfries and Nithsdale. This would have been ideal if nothing more than a line between Carlisle and Glasgow had been

contemplated; but the Grand Junction Railway, which was the moving spirit behind the English end of the enterprise, had plans for a considerably wider field of activity, and a route up Annandale was chosen instead. This brought the Caledonian into conflict with the G.P.K. &A. people; an independent route to the south was projected, and from 1847 the name Glasgow and South Western Railway was taken. The emblem of the G.P.K.&A. was adopted, because it was equally appropriate to the enlarged company. The three devices banded together by the crown are the wand of Mercury, symbolizing the carrying of traffic; the distaff, associated with Minerva the goddess of handicrafts, symbolizing the industries of the country served by the railway; and the trident of Neptune, symbolizing the connection with various ports on the Ayrshire coast. The Glasgow and South Western Railway later became a very successful operator of steamship services in the Firth of Clyde.

43 **Picnic Saloon;** London and North Western Railway.

In these days of private motoring it is difficult at times to appreciate what travelling conditions were like in Victorian times, especially when it came to holidays and other pleasure outings. With large families travelling for a month's stay at the sea, or in Scotland, the transport arrangements were a major problem and for the convenience of such parties the majority of railways constructed saloon carriages that could be hired by private individuals, and conveyed from the home station to any destination. These saloons were mostly six-wheelers, and included separate accommodation for the family servants and ample room for luggage. In the summer holiday season many of these saloons would be in use, and there is a recorded occasion on the Highland Railway when the 7.50 a.m. train from Perth included private saloons from the London and North Western, Midland, and Great Northern Railways, and no fewer than *thirteen* different horseboxes. Even before the end of the nineteenth century the demand for private saloons for night travel was on the decline, with the general introduction of comfortable sleeping-cars with private berths on the night expresses, and the North Western converted some of their saloons for purely day use, and renamed them 'Picnic Saloons'. Our picture shows one of these interesting little coaches – a period piece not only in railway carriage construction, but as a reminder of the changing trends of railway travel requirements.

44 **Chariot-ended first-class carriage;** Highland Railway.

The Highland Railway was for many years distinguished by the spartan character of its passenger carriages, and the four-wheeled third-class vehicles used on the Inverness–Wick trains were only 25 ft. long and barely 8 ft. wide. Into those carriages were crammed seats for 50 passengers. The local people took this kind of thing as the ordinary way of travelling by train. Anything more luxurious would have been regarded as degenerate, or 'going soft'. The first-class carriages were naturally more spacious, and our picture illustrates one of the so-called 'chariot-ended' vehicles. The end compartments had seats on one side only and glass end panels. They were slightly shorter than the five-compartment 'thirds', but due to the more lavish nature of the accommodation they seated only 20 passengers. Even with this concession the journey from Inverness to Wick must have been something of an ordeal in four-wheeled non-corridor carriages, with none of the amenities of modern travel. The through trains took about 8 hours to cover the 160 miles, with stops at most stations. For many years the refreshment room at Bonar Bridge used to do a brisk trade in soup and hard-boiled eggs, at whatever time of the day the trains saw fit to arrive. They were often very much behind schedule. The green livery was standard except for a period between 1897 and 1907, when the upper panels of the coaches were painted white.

45 **Composite four-wheeled carriage;** Somerset and Dorset Joint Railway.
The Somerset and Dorset began its existence through the amalgamation of two very small local lines, and much of its business remained quite local and tuned to the leisurely tempo of life in a wholly rural community. Before it became a joint concern with the Midland and the London and South Western as equal partners, the initials 'S.&D.' were often interpreted as 'Slow and Dirty'! While in later years the line never exactly blossomed forth as one of the high-speed routes of this country any stimga of dirtiness vanished, and the highly distinctive blue engines and carriages were beautifully maintained. The coach in our picture, a composite of late Victorian times, is unusually spacious in its accommodation, and in addition to the handsome lining out in black and gold the coach carries the company's coat of arms, embodying the arms of the city of Bath, and of the town of Dorchester. When to the original line, meandering through exceedingly rural farming country, from Wimborne, via Wincanton and Glastonbury to Highbridge, there was added the line over the Mendips to Bath, coaches like that in our picture were confined to the slow local trains, and some pleasant bogie stock – albeit non-corridor – was built for the new line (see reference 133). But the four-wheelers represented perfect little period pieces, representative of the days when railways provided virtually the only means of travel in the rural communities.

46 **Family Saloon;** London Chatham and Dover Railway.
This picturesque little carriage, which dates from 1881, is typical of the many types of family saloon built for hire to private family parties. At first sight it would seem strange to find doors labelled 'first' and 'second'; but the door marked 'second' led into a fairly narrow compartment of the ordinary type wherein travelled the family servants. There were seats for at least six of them, on nicely upholstered though rather narrow seats, and the windows were curtained. A door from the middle of this compartment led into the main saloon. Next to the servants compartment was the section reserved for luggage, while at the opposite end was a compartment almost as large as the servants 'second' in which there were to be found all the necessary toilet facilities. All that was lacking in this little self-contained saloon were the means of cooking, or even boiling water. On the London Chatham and Dover Railway itself, however, journeys were not expected to last very long, though these private saloons were apt to be hired for journeys extending far beyond the confines of the owning railway. Some saloons included cupboards for crockery, though the carrying of this was inclined to be a hazardous business when saloons were being shunted from one train to another. An old friend who used to travel to Scotland in one of these saloons once said to me: 'We did wish that the crockery was the railway company's, and not ours!'

47 **'L' class 4-4-0 locomotive;** South Eastern and Chatham Railway.
The fusion of the former South Eastern, and London Chatham and Dover Railways in 1898 under a single Managing Committee did not amalgamate the two companies in a financial sense, but it produced unification of traffic operation and all engineering matters, and the partnership of H. S. Wainwright as

Locomotive Superintendent with Robert Surtees as Chief Draughtsman resulted in a range of beautiful and successful locomotives. The design for a new express passenger type – a powerful superheater 4-4-0 – was completed just at the time of Wainwright's death, but orders for it had not then been placed. The new locomotive engineer was R. E. L. Maunsell, formerly of the Great Southern and Western Railway, in Ireland; but apart from some changes in the detail of the valve gear he accepted the design as prepared by Surtees. The year was 1914. The new engines were urgently needed, but neither the company's works at Ashford nor any British manufacturer could give the quick delivery required, and the order for the first batch was given to the German firm of A. Borsig of Berlin. The engines were shipped in parts and erected at Ashford, and there was a flavour of the dramatic about this work because Borsig's men were engaged upon it to within a few weeks before the outbreak of war with Germany in August 1914. Ironically enough, one of the first duties of the new engines was to work troop-trains in connection with the war. They proved excellent, hard-working and long-lived engines, and all of them survived to do good work through the *second* world war. They were the first S.E.&C.R. engines to have the less-ornate livery in which all the elaborate lining and ornamental brasswork was abandoned. Our picture shows the class as it ran originally in 1914. In later years the livery became even more sombre – one of plain dull grey.

48 **A Continental boat train carriage;** South Eastern and Chatham Railway.

The boat expressses of the S.E.&C.R. were most foreigners' first introduction to England, and great importance was attached to the provision of first-class rolling stock. In the early years of the twentieth century there was no comparison between the accommodation provided in England and France. Across the Channel, although the speeds run between Calais and Paris were much higher than on the S.E.&C.R., the journey was performed more often than not in dingy six-wheelers, and the riding was usually rough and uncomfortable. The S.E.&C.R. trains were made up of excellent bogie carriages, though at that time they were not vestibuled throughout. Some Pullman cars were included in the make-up, but most of the stock was non-corridor, though plentifully provided with lavatories. Our picture shows a tri-composite carriage, on which the roof board reads 'Continental Express London & Folkestone'. In this carriage, with two compartments for each of the three classes, there was seating for 10 first-class, 14 second-, and 16 third-class passengers. The boat train runs, whether to Folkestone or Dover, lasted only a few minutes over 1½ hours, and in those far-off days there were no such things as Custom examinations at the ports. England was then a free-trade country and one stepped straight down from train to boat, and departure took place in a very short time.

49 **Drummond's 'double-single' No. 720;** London and South Western Railway.

The idea that the coupling of the driving wheels of a locomotive impaired its free qualities died very hard on the railways of Britain. On the Great Northern Railway that great Scottish engineer Patrick Stirling built none but single-driver locomotives for express work, but one would hardly have expected his brother Scot, Dugald Drummond, to have cherished any of the same ideas. He had built very successful four-coupled engines for both the North British and the Caledonian Railways, though at the same time it must be recalled that it was his one and only Caledonian single-wheeler,

No. 123 (reference 12), that had performed so well between Carlisle and Edinburgh in the Race to the North, in 1888. Be that as it may, his first express passenger engine for the London and South Western was a four-cylinder machine with the two sets of cylinders driving separate axles. Engine No. 720 was completed at Nine Elms works in 1897. The first boiler fitted to this engine was not large enough to supply steam to *four* cylinders, and not only were the cylinders lined up to reduce their diameter by no less than 2½ in. – from 16½ to 14 in. – but a much larger boiler was fitted, and in this guise No. 720 became the exceedingly handsome engine shown in our picture. She was a swift runner but, it must be admitted, no faster than Drummond's four-coupled and six-coupled passenger engines. She had a skilful regular driver, Geare by name, who knew all her little peculiarities, and took an immense pride in her turnout. But No. 720 was an odd engine – the only one of her kind. There were five other four-cylinder uncoupled eight-wheelers on the L.S.W.R.; but these five had smaller boilers, and could not compete in performance with No. 720.

50 **Main-line carriage;** London and South Western Railway.
One can appreciate the policy of the South Eastern and Chatham Railway in having none but non-corridor carriages on even the finest of its express train services; but it is remarkable to recall that the same practice prevailed over the greater part of the London and South Western system which, of course, had much longer journeys to perform. It is true that on the principal services to the far west – to Plymouth, North Devon and North Cornwall – some corridor trains were run with restaurant cars; but until after the end of World War I the popular express trains to Bournemouth and Weymouth were made up entirely of non-corridor coaches. Of course there was a strong practical reason for using non-corridor coaches as much as possible. One could convey many more passengers for the same dead weight of carriage, and thus the loads hauled by the locomotives could be kept down, and the cost of running the trains not excessive. A single comparison will make this point clear. Before the war the load of the fast 2 p.m. express from Waterloo to Bournemouth was about 270 tons – entirely non-corridor. After the war, with a train vestibuled throughout the load was usually at least 320 tons. Non-corridor carriages remained in use on the Bournemouth trains for many years after the war, and in the early 1920s I made many journeys in vehicles of this kind – not very attractive for a run of 2½ hours.

51–52 **Early semaphore signals and box;** Stewarts Lane Junction.
In the earliest days of railways pointsmen were employed, stationed at the actual junction, to pull the points over by hand as and when required. As the speed of trains increased it was necessary to give drivers some prior indication of whether it was safe to proceed, and on which route, and at a number of places a semaphore type of indicator was installed. It then became desirable to include some mechanism to prevent the wrong signal being lowered, and this led to the development of interlocking between the levers controlling the points and those controlling the signals. It was then a logical step to put the levers all together, and provide a shelter for the man working them, and in such a way the earliest signal boxes were developed. These boxes, like the famous one at Stewarts Lane Junction, Battersea, shown in our picture, had all the associated signals carried on masts extending above the roof of the box. These signals told a driver whether he must stop or proceed, and it was left to his experience and judgment

as to *where* he should stop, if the signals indicated so. For instance, if his line converged with another one he was expected to stop short of the other line, so that his locomotive would not foul the path of another train. It was soon found necessary, however, to erect the semaphore signal at the exact spot where he was required to stop. This necessitated wire connections from the signal box to the post and made things more complicated from the viewpoint of signal engineering. But this development greatly lessened the chance of any misjudgment of distance by the driver, and with increasing density and speed of traffic it was essential. Picturesque old signal boxes, like that at Stewarts Lane, lost the arrays of signals carried on their roofs, for all the semaphores became fixed at specific points in the layout. The signal box at Stewarts Lane was the trade-mark of the famous signalling firm of Saxby and Farmer Ltd., one of the pioneers of the art of interlocking, and thus of the safety features so essential to the working of railways.

53–54 **Brunel's disc and crossbar signal;** Great Western Railway.
In the pioneer days of railways each engineer seemed to have his own ideas as to the equipment needed for operating the traffic. There was little in the way of consultation towards standard practice, and one has only to look at these Great Western signals and to recall that they were in use at the same time as the Stewart's Lane signal box to realize how divergent the practices of different railways were. But in almost every respect the Great Western did things differently from everyone else. In the gauge of its track, in the form of its permanent way and in the design of its locomotives it stood apart. Its great Chief Engineer, I. K. Brunel, the great protagonist of the broad gauge, invented the very distinctive disc and crossbar type of signal, which in one respect was much in advance of some contemporaries. In some forms of semaphore, when 'all clear' was indicated the arm dropped down into a slot inside the post and became invisible. Unfortunately the same indication could have been given if the connections had broken, or the arm had fallen off completely. It was not a positive indication. Brunel's was vastly better in principle, for by rotating the mechanism on a vertical axis the disc was displayed to the driver to indicate stop, while something quite different – the crossbar shown broadside on – indicated all clear. By modern ideas it was a crude, cumbersome arrangement; but the principles were sound enough. Life was strenuous for the maintenance men in those old days. Nothing so luxurious as a ladder was provided for them to climb to attend to the lamps, or oil the bearings. Small notches were cut in the post to provide a foothold, and with no more help than this the maintenance man had to climb to the top of a post which in some cases might be 40 ft. or 50 ft. high!

Alongside the disc and crossbar in our picture is shown one of the 'Fantails', or 'Ten Minute Signals', which were used on the Great Western Railway for more than 20 years. These boards, like the disc and crossbar, were rotated on a vertical axis, and were the forerunners of the modern semaphore 'distant' signal. The 'Fantails' had *three* positions. One side was painted red, and if this were displayed it meant 'stop'; the 'green', as shown in the picture, meant 'caution', and that a driver must travel slowly; but when no message was to be conveyed the board was turned to the third position, namely edge-on.

55 **West Coast Joint Stock coat of arms.**
The origin of the West Coast Joint Stock, operated by the London and North Western and Caledonian Railways, has been referred to under reference 28. Although the so-called West Coast route

begins at Euston the 'joint stock' was used only on Anglo-Scottish expresses, and it included passenger vehicles, dining-cars and sleeping-cars, and all kinds of postal and passenger luggage-vans. The emblem – for one could hardly call it a 'coat of arms' – was in keeping with the style of the two companies concerned. The North Western took Britannia as its emblem, and the Caledonian, the Royal arms of Scotland. The West Coast Joint Stock had nothing more nor less than the lion of Scotland, set off with some pleasant ornamentation including the rose and the thistle. The name 'West Coast' was strictly speaking much of a misnomer, because it was only for a brief 2 miles north of Lancaster and again at the Solway Firth that the line came in sight of the sea. In Scotland, indeed, if the journey in a 'W.C.J.S.' vehicle was being continued to Aberdeen, the line crossed the country and for the last 16 miles was running close beside the *east* coast, in full view of the North Sea! But in so far as the route was the most westerly of the three trunk routes from London to Scotland the name 'West Coast' was justified.

56 **East Coast Joint Stock coat of arms.**

The East Coast route to Scotland, in which the Great Northern, North Eastern, and North British Railways were partners, first approached the actual coast at Alnmouth, Northumberland. But after that it became truly a coastal route, and there were not many stretches between that station and Montrose when the line was far from the sea. Oddly enough, however, the last 38 miles of the journey to Aberdeen from Kinnaber Junction were made by the exercising of running powers over the metals of the Caledonian, and thus over the *West* Coast route. The East Coast Joint Stock coat of arms is a pleasing example of a gartered emblem, including the three lions from the Royal arms of England; the lion of Scotland, and in the two lower quarters the arms of the cities of Edinburgh (left) and London (right). Again the ornamentation includes the rose and the thistle. It is of interest to note that the two upper quarters of the shield later formed the centrepiece of the Great Northern coat of arms used from 1910 onwards. Although a purely English railway, the G.N.R. in this later design thus took the lions of both England and Scotland, and included also the thistle and the rose. The Great Northern may not have been the largest or the richest partner in the East Coast alliance; but it was always unquestionably the pace-maker, and in its coat of arms of later years it proclaimed, for all the world to see, that its interests lay as much in Scotland as in England.

57 **The Royal Mail coat of arms;** Travelling Post Offices.

All travelling post office vans carry the Royal arms of the United Kingdom of Great Britain and Northern Ireland, and in showing this beautiful device in our picture it is appropriate to refer back more than three centuries in history to find how the postal system of this country became the 'Royal Mail'. The times of the Tudor monarchs were troubled. England had only just emerged from the carnage and misery of the Wars of the Roses. Bitter feelings remained. Intrigue was rife, and many means of communication were surreptitiously practised. The threat of the Armada compelled a tightening up, and the posts were brought under the control of the Crown. But for some time many unofficial postal systems continued, offering conveyance at cheaper rates. These had to be suppressed by law, and eventually in the years 1635–51 a system of mail routes and post towns covered the whole of England, and one route across the Border, from Berwick via Dunbar to Edinburgh, was organized by one Thomas Witherings, with Government authority. But the postal service was to undergo many vicissitudes before the picturesque system of Royal Mail coaches and galloping postboys was firmly established, and in 1830 a start was made in transferring the conveyance of mails to the new railways. In 1838 the first travelling post office with the Royal arms on its central door went into service on the Grand Junction Railway. Since that time T.P.O. carriages have been operated on many routes, and there are now two exclusively postal trains – one from Euston to Glasgow and Aberdeen, and one from Paddington to Penzance.

58 **The Great North of Scotland Railway coat of arms.**
This little railway with the high-sounding title actually operated only in the north-eastern corner. It was promoted with the idea of making a railway from Aberdeen to Inverness; but owing to financial difficulties and a good deal of bad management it never got farther from Aberdeen than Elgin. Indeed it reached that northern burgh only after the Highland Railway had struck first, and secured the most direct route through the hilly country eastwards from Elgin to Keith. But from a bad start, and after passing through a long period of bad relations with its neighbour railways, the 'Great North', to which its name was frequently abbreviated, developed into a smart and efficient concern. Although most of its interests lay north of Aberdeen, in through connections to Inverness and farther north and in the fisheries of the north-east coast, it had the important Deeside branch to Ballater, under regular Royal patronage for the annual visit of the Queen, and later her son, and her grandson, to Balmoral. There may have been ambitions to reach Inverness and to extend beyond into the Western Highlands; but Aberdeen was the nodal point of the system and it is the city arms of Aberdeen, the three silver towers, that figure in two out of the four quarters of its shield. The alternate quarters bear the lion rampant of Scotland. It is definitely known that this design was never registered at the College of Heralds, nor submitted to Lord Lyon. Had it been submitted one feels that it would have stood a strong chance of rejection, through use of part of the Royal arms of Scotland. In this, however, it was no more unorthodox than the coats of arms of the Caledonian, of the London and North Western, and of the West Coast Joint Stock.

59 **The '1020' class 4-4-0 locomotive;** Great Central Railway.
The extension of the one-time Manchester, Sheffield and Lincolnshire Railway from Annesley, in north Nottinghamshire, through to London in 1899, and its assumption of the title of Great Central Railway, was followed by a period of intense activity in search of new traffics. The new line had to fight on all fronts, and its campaign was waged by the introduction of very fast and comfortable trains, lavishly equipped with restaurant and buffet cars. And although passengers were not many at first, the company needed to be ready for expansion. In June 1900 John G. Robinson was appointed Locomotive Engineer and he embarked upon a programme of building large and powerful new locomotives. Really they were too large for the traffic that then existed; but the policy was pursued of being ready for any development. The '1020' class, as it can conveniently be called, was introduced at the end of 1901. It was at once distinguished by its very graceful proportions. It seemed as though an almost loving care had been lavished upon every detail of the design, from the handsomely shaped chimney, to the sweeping curve of the driving-wheel splashers and to the canopied cab. The painting was tastefully done, with the basic rich dark green set off by the dark

purple-red underframes and the use of the company's new coat of arms on both engine and tender. These engines were not merely good to look at; they were capable of hard work at high speed, and by 1905 they were running the 103 miles between Marylebone and Leicester in 105 minutes. These engines, good though they were, proved no more than a curtain-raiser to Mr. Robinson's programme of engine building; but as the locomotives that inaugurated the fast services on the London extension line they have a special place in railway history.

60 **Vestibuled clerestory carriage;** Great Central Railway.
There were no half-measures about the Great Central extension to London. The line was engineered so as to permit full-speed running throughout from Leicester to the point where it joined the Metropolitan Railway north of Aylesbury. Even the smallest country stations were laid out in the most spacious manner, and the train services were operated with sets of splendid new carriages. The Great Central adopted the slogan, so far as its London trains were concerned: 'every express train vestibuled throughout, with buffet or restaurant car'. This was, in modern parlance, 'quite something' in 1900. The old-established main lines from Kings Cross and Euston were introducing new corridor coaches in a big way at that time; but if extra coaches were required on a train those extras were more often than not non-corridor, and six-wheelers into the bargain. The Great Central also changed their liveries, both of engines and carriages. The Manchester, Sheffield and Lincolnshire, like its ally the Great Northern, had carriages finished in plain varnished teak; but the Great Central at first adopted the very smart two-tone scheme of grey and dark brown. These coaches were adorned with no fewer than *three* coats of arms on each side. The set trains used on the London extension usually consisted of five of these handsome new carriages; but as one observer commented, the new trains were 'too smart to be recognized', and after a few years the G.C.R. reverted to varnished teak.

61 **Ivatt 4-2-2 locomotives;** Great Northern Railway.
Until the death of Patrick Stirling the G.N.R. had used single-driver express locomotives to the exclusion of all others on the principal expresses, but his successor, H. A. Ivatt, began immediately to build larger engines of the 4-4-0 and 4-4-2 types. Train loads were very much on the increase, and greater adhesion was required for rapid starting, and climbing of the long gradients en route. In view of this change of policy it was therefore something of a surprise when Ivatt himself built a bogie single-driver express locomotive in 1898 and continued during the years 1900–1 until there were 12 of them in service. The early 1900s were a period of intense competition between the various independent companies, and particularly in respect of the London services to and from Leeds and Bradford the G.N.R. was being hard pressed by the Midland. The Great Northern reply was to put on some lightly-loaded high-speed trains, and for these the new Ivatt single-wheelers were ideal. These engines were not only light-load machines. For many years the 5.30 p.m. dining-car express from Kings Cross to Newcastle was worked by an engine of this type between Grantham and York, with a load of 200 tons, and their timekeeping was always good. These engines also had the melancholy distinction of being scrapped *en bloc*. Usually engines are withdrawn one by one, as their useful work-life is finished, or when deterioration of the frames has gone beyond repair. But these Ivatt singles were deemed obsolete in 1918, lined up in a single long line at Doncaster, and the whole class scrapped

at a single blow, as it were. They were excellent engines in their day.

62 **Clerestory brake composite carriage;** Great Northern Railway.
The G.N.R., like its great rival from Euston, was somewhat reluctant to employ large bogie coaches; but when the time came for changing old policies it was done in no half-hearted way. The new stock used on the mid-day Anglo-Scottish express from July 1897 was truly magnificent, both from its sheer size and for the splendour of its appointments. The traditional livery of varnished teak remained, but on these tremendously long coaches, with their six-wheeled bogies and high clerestory roofs, it looked superb. The coach chosen for illustration is a brake composite – a self-contained suite of compartments for use as a single through coach running to some destination not served by the main train, and containing accommodation for first- and third-class passengers, and space for their heavy luggage and a seat for a guard, or a travelling inspector. These fine carriages were used on the Leeds trains in addition to the Scottish expresses, and on the through Kings Cross–Manchester service, which the G.N.R. operated in partnership with the Great Central via Retford and Sheffield. Like many picturesque features of the British steam railways these clerestory carriages were expensive to construct, and after Mr. Gresley had become Carriage Superintendent – he who afterwards achieved such fame as a locomotive designer, and a knighthood in recognition of it – the design of Great Northern carriages was changed to have a much simpler design of roof (see reference 65).

63 **12-Wheeled dining car;** West Coast Joint Stock.
One of the earliest London and North Western essays into the design of dining cars has already been described and illustrated (reference 30). The clerestory type of roof was employed probably to give additional daylight and ventilation in the roof. But whether this was the true reason, or not, the clerestory type of roof remained standard for all L.N.W.R. dining cars until the introduction of the 'American Specials', for working between Euston and Liverpool Riverside. All dining cars on the Anglo-Scottish services were clerestory roofed, and beautiful vehicles they were. At the turn of the century, and for many years after, an express train on the L.N.W.R. usually had a most variegated appearance so far as coaches were concerned. Old flat-roofed corridor and non-corridor vehicles were interspersed with newer types with high elliptical roofs; and in the midst of a long cavalcade would come one or two dining cars with clerestory roofs. In 1908 there were built at Wolverton works the splendid new 12-wheeled coaches for the afternoon Scottish expresses, and on these – at long last – one could have seen a perfect uniformity in coach styles, but for one thing; the dining cars in these new sets were still of the clerestory-roofed type. They remained so well into the days of the L.M.S.R. when these beautiful Anglo-Scottish trains were painted in Midland red. The North Western, and W.C.J.S. 12-wheeled dining cars represented a peak of achievement in railway carriage building, in the craftsmanship put into their construction and the perfect smoothness of the riding. Even in these days I have never known anything better.

64 **Third-class dining cars;** Midland Railway.
The Midland Railway carriage works at Derby, like those of the North Western at Wolverton, were past-masters in the art of building beautiful carriages, though the policy of the company so far as dining cars were concerned varied considerably up to the early years of the present century. On the Scottish trains the cars were

vestibuled and connected to the rest of the train, whereas on certain highly-favoured Manchester expresses the dining cars were separate. Passengers wishing to dine travelled throughout in the car, and could not pass to any other part of the train even if they wished. The car illustrated, which was one allocated to purely internal services on the Midland Railway, was one of a group introduced by David Bain in the early 1900s. The ends were of normal Midland profile, but throughout the length of the actual dining saloon the body was bellied out, and earned for these cars the name of 'clipper sided'. Some similar cars were allocated to the joint Scotch services worked with the Glasgow and South Western and North British Railways. The coaches on the St. Pancras–Glasgow trains were lettered 'M.&G.S.W.' and those on the Edinburgh trains 'M.&N.B.' As with the West Coast Joint Stock all this joint Scottish stock on the Midland route was of Midland design and built at Derby. In contrast to the West Coast trains the Scottish expresses by the Midland route were entirely uniform in appearance, all having the same profile of clerestory roof. There were differences between the Clayton and the Bain coaches in the shape of the windows, and ventilators above the doors; but these were points for the connoisseur rather than the casual observer. Another is that during this period in the early 1900s the Midland never used the term Dining Car; whether first or third class they were always 'Dining Carriages'.

65 **Bow-ended elliptical-roofed dining car;** Great Northern Railway.
Yet another contrast in dining-car styles is to be seen in this fine example of a 12-wheeler from the Great Northern works at Doncaster – in this case titled a 'Dining Saloon'. On long distance express trains on which many passengers would be taking meals, it was the practice on all the three Anglo-Scottish routes to run dining cars in pairs. One coach would be devoted entirely to third-class passengers, as in the Midland example, reference 64, and the other, as in this Great Northern example, would include a smaller saloon and also the kitchen, which would serve both saloons. On the North Western dining cars in pairs were run on the Liverpool, Manchester and Holyhead trains. On the Anglo-Scottish trains single composite dining cars were run separately in the Glasgow and Edinburgh sections of the trains. This Great Northern example illustrated the carriage-building style introduced at Doncaster by Mr. H. N. Gresley, with its bow-ended elliptical roofs. This was a style that persisted throughout Gresley's tenure of office on both the Great Northern and the London and North Eastern Railways. The latest examples of the style were fully air-conditioned coaches built for the Flying Scotsman trains as recently as 1938, in which the characteristic, highly varnished, teak panelling persisted to the end. The Great Northern cars, of which one is illustrated, were distinguished in the first-class saloons by their curtained windows, green leather upholstery, and the pink lampshades on the tables.

66 **Composite 70-ft. Dining Car;** Great Western Railway.
G. J. Churchward, Locomotive Carriage and Wagon Superintendent of the G.W.R., and later Chief Mechanical Engineer, not only built exceedingly powerful and efficient locomotives but displayed equal skill in designing carriages in which the maximum number of passengers could be conveyed in comfort for a given dead weight. Under reference 138 is a description of one of the earliest 70-ft. coaches, in which accommodation for 80 passengers was provided for a dead weight of only 33 tons. The dining car shown in this picture was one of the vehicles included in the new stock of the year 1923, when the older clipper-sided

bodies, with recessed doors, had given place to smooth, steel-panelled exteriors. The elaborate lining of old was nevertheless fully restored on these coaches, in which a return was made to the old chocolate and cream livery, after a period when G.W.R. coaching stock was finished in the lake livery shown in reference 138. On trains like the Cornish Riviera Express and the Torbay Limited only a single car was run, including both first- and third-class accommodation, and a kitchen between. On the sharply-timed Great Western services weight could not be spared for running a pair of dining cars, as on certain L.N.W.R. and Great Northern services, and on West of England expresses at busy times it was quite normal to serve three sittings of lunch.

67 **The Hughes 4-6-4 tank engines;** L.M.S.R.
After the grouping of the railways in 1923 George Hughes, formerly Chief Mechanical Engineer of the Lancashire and Yorkshire Railway, was appointed to the same post on the L.M.S.R. and in 1924 he built a tank engine version of his 4-cylinder 4-6-0 passenger engine – the 'Lanky Dreadnoughts' as they were known on former L.N.W.R. lines. In their machinery and boilers the 4-6-4 tanks were the same as the 4-6-0 main-line engines, but they were intended for heavy short-distance hauls in the hilly districts north-east of Manchester. They worked to Blackburn and Burnley, while one or two of them were tried on the heavily graded Buxton line of the former L.N.W.R. Unlike most passenger tank engines of the period, they never carried the L.M.S.R. standard livery of Midland red. They never had L.&Y.R. numbers, but were L.M.S. 11110–11119 from the outside. Most of them ran throughout their short lives in plain unlined black, and only three of them were at any time painted red. As will be appreciated from our picture, they were massive-looking and handsome engines; but they were rather too massive, and too expensive to maintain for the duties they worked. Four cylinders, and their attendant valve gear was certainly a complication for a short-distance tank engine, and they were displaced from their special duties after the introduction of the '2300' class 2-6-4 tanks (reference 175).

68 **Adams 0-6-2 radial tank engine;** North Staffordshire Railway.
Among the local railways of Great Britain the North Staffordshire was at the same time one of the oldest and one of the busiest. It had the teeming industrial districts of the Potteries virtually to itself, while enjoying a very useful alliance with the London and North Western whereby certain of the through expresses between London and Manchester travelled via Stoke and Macclesfield, and were hauled between Stoke and Manchester by North Staffordshire engines. The appointment of Adams as Locomotive Superintendent in 1902 marked the beginning of the modern era in North Stafford motive power, and the engine which is the subject of our picture belongs to a class of powerful general-service tank engines first introduced in 1903. They were primarily designed for heavy goods traffic, and had coupled wheels of only 5 ft. 0 in. diameter. For their day they were powerful units, and proved extremely useful in all kinds of local traffic in the Potteries, goods and passenger alike. There is, however, an occasion on record when one of them, engine No. 158, was called upon for a much more arduous duty. The North Staffordshire Railway always worked the heavy and important 12.5 p.m. express from Manchester to Euston, as far as Stoke, and one of the large 0-6-4 tanks was assigned to this duty. But one day a defect developed in the regular engine, and the only substitute available in Manchester

was one of the 0-6-2 'radials'. This small engine had to tackle a substantial corridor dining-car train of 310 tons, but was driven and fired with such skill that the loss of time between Stockport and Stoke-on-Trent was trifling. Speed reached a maximum of 53½ m.p.h. on level track – quite a remarkable feat for a small local tank engine with a heavy express train.

69 **4-6-2 Express tank engine;** London and North Western Railway.
The successful application of superheating to the main-line express passenger engines of Crewe design led to the introduction of tank engines for fast passenger working in which the greatly reduced coal and water consumption, consequent upon superheating, would permit of a greater sphere of activity than that usually associated with tank engines, and would release tender engines for other duties. These fine 4-6-2 engines, first introduced at the end of 1910 were generally similar in the design of their machinery to the main-line passenger engines, but they had a variation in the layout of the Joy valve gear, using direct instead of indirect motion, which was later applied to the 'Prince of Wales' class express passenger 4-6-0s. The 4-6-2 tank engines had coupled wheels 5 ft. 8½ in. diameter, and from the outset they did excellent work on the longer-distance residential trains from London and Manchester. They were particularly effective on the heavily-graded line up to Buxton. One of their most interesting early duties was on the Central Wales line from Shrewsbury through Llandrindod Wells to Swansea. In later years some of them were transferred to the Northern Division, where they worked local trains on the Windermere branch, and put in some hard work as bank engines between Tebay and Shap Summit. The huge initials on the side tanks of No. 2665 were not used for very long. Like the 4-4-2 non-superheated 'Precursor' tanks they always carried the initials of the Company, but in a rather more modest size. The coloured picture was prepared from an official photograph and is curious in that for this short period the normal policy of the L.N.W.R., in not displaying the Company's name at all, was so blatantly reversed.

70 **0-4-4 Passenger tank engine;** Midland Railway.
To those who knew the Midland Railway in its later days, and equally the Midland division of the L.M.S.R., the 0-4-4 passenger tank engines were such familiar objects and so regularly entrusted to hard and important local duties that it is difficult to recall that the design originated as long ago as 1875. Moreover, the majority of the engines retained their outward appearance practically unchanged for more than 60 years. Liveries changed, of course. Until 1884 the standard Midland colour was green, with black and white lining. Then came the famous Derby red. The tank engines were not finished in so ornate a style. Many of them did not carry the Company's initials and the number was displayed in raised brass figures in the middle of the side tanks. Then came the style shown in our picture, which was followed by the L.M.S.R. red. The inevitable black followed, and finally a few of them survived into national ownership. In their hey-day there were no fewer than 205 of them in service, with numbers running from 1226 to 1430, and they worked all over the Midland system except over the Settle and Carlisle line. They were familiar enough engines around Leeds and Bradford, and some of them worked westwards from Skipton to Lancaster and Morecambe. In 1949 there were still 53 of them at work, but by that time most of them had been rebuilt, with new boilers having Belpaire fireboxes and plain-topped domes. With the passing of the picturesque original

domes with Salter type safety valves mounted on them, and the beautifully shaped brass safety valve column over the firebox, much of their distinctive character disappeared; but their longevity is a tribute to the excellence of their mechanical design and of the workmanship put into their construction.

71 **Great Northern Railway coat of arms.**

This was probably the most elaborate emblem adopted by any of the British Railways, though some overseas administrations that were at one time strongly under British influence even exceeded the Great Northern in their comprehensiveness and ornamentation. Our reproduction of the device of the G.N.R. gives no impression of its size. Actually it was about twice the extent of the more normal coat of arms, and in its rich colouring it looked magnificent on the varnished teak carriages. It was not displayed on locomotives. In writing of the East Coast Joint Stock (reference 56) I, mentioned how the Great Northern was the pacemaker of the alliance. The interest of the company in Scotland is shown prominently on its own emblem with the thistle as prominent as the rose near the top, coming immediately below the arms of the City of London. Though the main business of the Great Northern came from the industries of Nottinghamshire and Yorkshire, London was always the main spring-board of its business enterprise, and on this heraldic device it fittingly crowns everything else. Three quartered shields are displayed beneath the thistle and the rose. The upper one has in its top quarters the three lions of England, and the lion rampant of Scotland, and below the arms of Huntingdon (left) and Peterborough. The leftward shield below symbolizes the one-time keen Great Northern interests to the west of its own main line, in association with the Great Central Railway. The arms are those of Grantham, Nottingham, Sheffield and Manchester. The rightward shield includes the Yorkshire centres of activity – Doncaster, Leeds, York and Bradford. Finally, at the bottom, in the centre, is the single shield carrying the arms of Wakefield. Two countries, twelve towns: such was the heraldic representation on the emblem of the Great Northern Railway. Sad to say, this device was abandoned after 1910 in favour of the smaller and less pretentious device mentioned in reference 56.

72 **Great Eastern Railway coat of arms.**

The line was an amalgamation of several smaller concerns operating in East Anglia, and it was one of the very few railways in England that enjoyed a monopoly in most of the territory it served. It is true that the Great Northern and the North Western penetrated into East Anglia as far as Cambridge, and north of Peterborough and March the Great Northern and the Great Eastern had certain important joint interests. Also the Midland and Great Northern Joint line cut across the northern part of Norfolk from King's Lynn to Cromer and Yarmouth. But elsewhere in East Anglia the Great Eastern had the field to itself and splendid service it rendered to the community. Its coat of arms was an assembly of the shields of eight cities and towns that it served, circled round the arms of the City of London, which again formed the centrepiece both businesswise and heraldically of the enterprise. The places represented round the perimeter are in some cases districts rather than centres of population, including the counties of Middlesex, Hertford, Huntingdon, and Northampton – all of which it penetrated. The towns represented are Cambridge, Ipswich, Maldon and Norwich. This again was a heraldic device that stemmed from earlier activities; otherwise one could be sure the important

Great Eastern associations with Lincoln and Yorkshire would have been symbolized, particularly in regard to the coal traffic from Doncaster and Mansfield areas, to East Anglia, and to the important north-country connections made at York. The Great Eastern once ran an express passenger service between London and York in opposition to the Great Northern, advertising the attractions of the 'Cathedral Route', travelling via Ely and Lincoln.

73 **Great Central Railway coat of arms.**

One naturally considers the Great Northern, the Great Eastern, and the Great Central together, because in the early years of the twentieth century their working arrangements were becoming so close that complete amalgamation was at one time seriously considered. The Great Central, as I have already emphasized under references 59 and 60, was a line that had to fight hard for existence after its audacious extension to London in 1899. Its coat of arms, so proudly and liberally displayed on engines and carriages alike, symbolized the speed and dash of the new organization. Crowning all was a locomotive, flanked with wings. The shield itself was a clever device, having at the top the arms of the three cities primarily served by its progenitor, the Manchester, Sheffield and Lincolnshire. Below is an adaptation of the familiar arms of the City of London, this time with two daggers instead of one – as a warning presumably of a readiness to fight! In the centre, what a railwayman with other sympathies once described to me as the 'flying bowler hat' (!) is the winged cap of Mercury, all incorporated to intensify the impression of speed. Most prominent, however, was the motto at the bottom – 'Forward'. This the Great Central certainly emulated, and in later years it became the motto of the London and North Eastern Railway, to which the men and traditions of the Great Central had much to contribute.

74 **North Eastern Railway coat of arms.**

Except for the mild incursion of the Hull and Barnsley Railway on its southern flank the North Eastern had a monopoly of the country between the Humber and the Tweed. With a huge traffic in coal, in relatively short hauls to the numerous small ports exporting to the Scandinavian countries and the Baltic, its revenue was at one time princely, and it could afford to take a more leisurely view of the passenger traffic flowing through its districts. So far as the East Coast service was concerned the Great Northern had sometimes to do not a little 'prodding' in order to get acceleration of the principal through trains. The North Eastern had two distinct coats of arms; the circular one shown in our picture, which was used on carriages and on the splashers of certain express locomotives, and a larger and more ornate device embodying the same three shields, and surrounded by a lot of decoration, which was displayed on engine tenders between the words NORTH and EASTERN. The large express locomotives, like the 'V' class Atlantic reference 117, thus included both varieties, the circular one on the driving-wheel splasher and the large one on the tender. In both devices York had the uppermost shield to itself. The other shields were those of two important constituents, to left, that of the Leeds Northern, and to right that of the York, Newcastle and Berwick. The former includes the city arms of Leeds, symbolic of the wool industry; the ship, typifying the maritime activities of Tees-side, and the other quarters representing industry and agriculture, rather than any particular places. The York, Newcastle and Berwick shield includes the arms of York in the first and fourth quarters,

Newcastle in the second, and Berwick in the third.

75 **Four-cylinder compound 4-4-0;** London and North Western Railway.
During his long career as Chief Mechanical Engineer of the L.N.W.R., F. W. Webb built a large number of compound locomotives at Crewe. His earlier types all had three cylinders, with two high-pressure cylinders outside, and one very large low-pressure cylinder between the frames. All his passenger engines on this system, including the eight-wheeled *Greater Britain* (reference 27) and the *Queen Empress* (reference 29) had the two pairs of driving wheels uncoupled, and there were times when differential slipping occurred. In his later designs, which were of the 4-4-0 wheel arrangement, all four cylinders drove on to the leading pair of coupled wheels and by this proper synchronization between the high- and low-pressure systems was secured. The engine illustrated, No. 1955 *Hannibal*, was built at Crewe in 1902, and was one of 40 units in the *Alfred the Great* class. They were powerful engines, and could handle heavy loads; but through a rather complicated arrangement of the valve gear, and low-pressure cylinders that were small in relation to the size of the high-pressure cylinders, they were not capable of any sustained high speed. At the time of their introduction there was a general move to accelerate all express passenger train services, and the 'Alfreds' unfortunately did not rise to the occasion. Webb's successor, George Whale, who took office in 1903, greatly improved them by providing them with a separately controlled valve gear for each set of cylinders. Even so, they were never very speedy engines, and their life on first-class express work was relatively short. Nevertheless, they represent an important stage in the evolution of British locomotive design, which inevitably had its setbacks, no less than its great successes.

76 **45-ft. Corridor 'brake-first';** West Coast Joint Stock.
It was in the Diamond Jubilee year, 1897, that the West Coast Companies put on the first all-corridor train running between England and Scotland – the famous 2 p.m. from Euston to Glasgow and Edinburgh, to which there were corresponding southbound departures from the Scottish cities. They were not the first all-corridor trains to run in this country; that distinction belongs to the Great Western Railway. But whereas the Birkenhead train from Paddington soon disappeared from prominence the West Coast trains became a perfect institution. To every railwayman up and down the line the 'two-o'clock' was always known as 'The Corridor', and the name lingered on well into L.M.S.R. days when the special stock built for it had been replaced by modern standard vehicles. The coach illustrated in our picture was of earlier build than the original stock of the corridor train of 1897, and dates from 1896. But it was similar in style and construction. The original 'Scotch' corridor trains had the following make-up:

For Glasgow: Third brake
Third corridor
Third dining car
First diner and kitchen
First diner
First corridor
For Edinburgh: Composite
Third brake
For Aberdeen: Composite
Third brake

All these coaches, although rather narrow by modern standards, were luxuriously appointed. The 'firsts' seated only two aside, and the 'thirds' three. It will also be seen from the make-up that a lavish amount of dining accommodation was provided.

77 **'Duke of Cornwall' class engine;** Great Western Railway.
Once the broad gauge had been abolished

in 1892 the Great Western management embarked upon a great plan of modernization and some fine new locomotives were built in large quantities at Swindon. In broad-gauge days the important junction of Newton Abbot had formed a divisional point between the fast-running sections of the West of England main line, and the very hilly and sharply curved line in South Devon and Cornwall. Engines were always changed at Newton Abbot, and at first the same practice was continued on the narrow gauge. Through expresses to the West came down from London behind the beautiful Dean 7 ft. 8 in. 4-2-2 singles and were taken forward by massive small-wheeled 4-4-0s of the 'Duke of Cornwall' class – usually known as the 'Dukes'. This class was first introduced in 1895, and 40 were built in the ensuing 2 years. Another 19 were added in 1899. They all had beautiful West Country names. Some were topographical, such as *St. Anthony*, *Tintagel*, *Eddystone*, *Mounts Bay*, others were of associations with the countryside such as *Cornubia*, *Tre*, *Pol*, *and Pen*, and *Cornishman*, while a few, including the one chosen for illustration, were of West Country characters in literature, such as *Amyas*, the very beautiful *Armorel*, *King Arthur* and *Sir Lancelot*. As motive power units the 'Dukes' were excellent engines, and after being displaced from regular passenger working in the West they still did much express work as bank engines assisting the newer machines whenever they needed help on the South Devon inclines. It was not unusual in the height of the summer to see one of the mighty 'King' class 4-6-0s piloted by a 'Duke'. After grouping, some of them were drafted to Central Wales and did good work on the former Cambrian line.

78 **Narrow gauge clerestory coach;** Great Western Railway.

At the turn of the century, when the new Dean 4-2-2 and 4-4-0 locomotives were setting up new standards of service on the narrow gauge Great Western lines, some excellent new carriages were also introduced, and our picture shows a 'composite' with the characteristic clerestory roof and the elaborate lining-out on the picturesque chocolate and cream basic livery. Great Western coaching-stock of that period was mounted on the Dean bogie, which was different from any other kind of bogie then in use. Reference has already been made (20) to the very good riding qualities of Midland bogie carriages. The suspension in these was adapted by T. G. Clayton from the American-built Pullman cars that were imported in 1874. The Great Western did not adopt this simple and successful design. Instead Dean brought out a design of his own, which had no centre at all, and the amount of sideplay was controlled by a peculiar method of suspension from the main frames. It proved very successful and was used on the Great Western for many years, until Churchward introduced his own design of bogie for the huge 70-ft. vehicles (reference 138). These Dean clerestory carriages had wooden centres to the wheels, built up in sections.

79 **A 6-ft. 'Castle' class 4-6-0;** Highland Railway.

In the year 1915 the Highland Railway had on order from Hawthorn Leslie and Co. Ltd., six 4-6-0 locomotives of a very powerful new design to be named after 'Rivers'. But by a combination of unfortunate circumstances they were not permitted to run on the Highland line, and they were sold to the Caledonian. To replace these engines orders were placed for further batches of well-tried existing designs: three of the 4-4-0 'Loch' class, for working on the Dingwall and Skye line which was carrying a very heavy wartime traffic, and three of the 4-6-0 'Castle' class, which had proved extremely reliable and hard working engines. The new engines, of which the *Brodie Castle* is shown in our picture, were not identical to earlier batches. The original design, first introduced in 1900 had 5 ft. 9 in., coupled wheels and the very small smokebox then typical of many engines of that period; in fact the length of the smokebox would seem to have been dictated by the size of the chimney – it was made just big enough to take the base of the chimney, and no more. A later batch of these engines had extended smokeboxes and certain changes in detail design. In the last three, ordered in 1916, the diameter of the coupled wheels was increased to 6 ft. 0 in., but there was one feature that the enginemen did not like at first, namely, the provision of a horizontal screw reversing gear in place of the steam reverser which had been traditional on the Highland Railway for many years. Because of the intense preoccupation of the North British Locomotive Company with war work, it was not until the year 1917 that the engines were delivered.

80 **Composite Corridor Carriage;** Highland Railway.

One naturally associates the Highland Railway with heavy tourist traffic in the summer holiday season, and with through carriage workings from England – so much so that some of the most important trains running between Perth and Inverness were composed almost entirely of 'foreign' stock, West Coast Joint, East Coast Joint, or Midland. Many of the purely Highland services were, even down to the time of grouping, worked with non-corridor trains, though bogie coaches had by then largely replaced the very spartan four-wheelers of the nineteenth century. But on the day trains of the Highland Railway the 'foreign' stock, from the North British and Caledonian Railways, did not provide all that was necessary and some fine corridor coaches were introduced just before the first world war, and built by Hurst, Nelson and Co. Ltd., of Motherwell. These, as shown in our picture, were finished in a handsome style of plain olive green exactly matching the locomotive style of the period as depicted on the 4-6-0 *Brodie Castle*. An attractive point of detail about the finish of these coaches was the shading of the bold block lettering, which was in emerald green. These carriages also had the Highland Railway coat of arms, displayed twice on both sides. At that time, although engines and carriages were painted the same colour, it would be rare to see an entirely green train. Almost every express would have some carriages from further afield in its make-up: Caledonian and North British on the day trains; W.C.J.S. on trains to and from England.

81 **'Scott' class 4-4-0 locomotive;** North British Railway.

The rivalry between the Caledonian and North British Railways will be referred to later (reference 102), and between 1900 and 1910 both were indulging in much publicity in their several ways. Until the turn of the century the Highland was the only Scottish railway which had persisted in the practice of naming its locomotives. The North British had a short spell during the time of Dugald Drummond, but in the flood-tide of publicity that accompanied the 'war' with the Caledonian it was resumed, and applied to all the principal express locomotive types. The 4-4-0s of the 'Scott' class were introduced in 1909 specially to work express trains between Edinburgh and Perth in connection with the Highland Railway. They were designed to use saturated steam, and were powerful locomotives for their day. But in 1914 an improved version of the class followed, equipped with superheaters, and it is one of these that is illustrated. They were all named after characters in the Waverley Novels, except for the first of the series, which was, of course, *Sir Walter Scott*. The earlier, and less powerful members of the class inevitably had the better known names, such as *Rob Roy*, *Red Gauntlet*, *Jeannie Deans*, and *The Fair Maid*. When it came to the superheater engines of 1914 there were some names that would have puzzled all but the most ardent of Sir Walter's 'fans', such as *Caleb Balderstone*, *Cuddie Headrigg* and *Dumbiedikes*; though equally there were some generally familiar ones, like *Kenilworth*, *Quentin Durward*, *The Talisman*, and the subject of our picture, *Claverhouse*.

82 **Non-corridor first-class carriage;** North British Railway.

At the present time one thinks either of corridor carriages for long distance travel or of diesel or electric multiple-unit trains for local or branch working, and the entire trend in recent years has been to build coaching stock in which the passengers could move about, either by means of the corridor, or through the passageways in the open saloon type of vehicle. In consequence one is apt to pass over a very interesting period in railway development when quite luxurious non-corridor stock was built for relatively short distance traffic. To represent the practice of the North British Railway, at a time when the 'Scott' class 4-4-0 locomotives of the super-heated variety were introduced, a very fine non-corridor first-class bogie coach has been chosen for illustration. The North British, in addition to its fast inter-city services and its participation in the East Coast services, operated some well-patronized local trains, used by season ticket holders working in Edinburgh and Glasgow, who would appreciate the comforts provided by carriages like the one shown in our picture. In addition to providing very comfortable accommodation these coaches, which were built by Hurst, Nelson and Co. Ltd., of Motherwell, were beautifully finished outside, with full lining and the N.B.R. coat of arms carried twice on each side of the vehicle.

83 **0-6-4 Passenger tank engines;** Midland Railway.

First among a group of four distinctive designs of passenger tank engines is R. M. Deeley's 0-6-4 of 1907, designed particularly for heavy coal traffic. It was in some ways a tank-engine version of the standard main-line goods locomotive, but provided with side tanks with a capacity of 2,250 gallons and a coal capacity of 3½ tons. This would enable engines of this class to run considerable mileages without refuelling, and in the operation of a heavy local service would cut to a minimum the time for shed duties needed between trips. Because of the unusual appearance of the side tanks these engines were nicknamed 'the flat-irons'. The large coal bunker in rear and the need to provide a trailing bogie instead of the more usual 0-6-2 type for local tank engines at that period made it necessary to give special attention to the suspension and bearings for all the wheels. The leading pair of wheels had the Cartazzi form of axle box, in order to permit of a degree of side play. Similarly, the joint in the coupling rods was equipped with spherical bearings to accommodate the side play in the leading coupled wheel axleboxes. Despite these special features the 'flat irons' were not very successful engines. They rode badly, and it was inadvisable to run them at any substantial speed, and they were eventually transferred to goods workings on which their tractive power could be utilized, but which needed no fast running.

84 **W. Pickersgill's 4-6-2 tank engine;** Caledonian Railway.

These handsome engines, of which 12 were built in 1917 by the North British Locomotive Co. Ltd., formed part of Pickersgill's general adoption of outside cylinders for large new locomotives, in contrast to the practice that had prevailed on the Caledonian since the days of Dugald Drummond. The fast trains from

Glasgow to the Clyde Coast stations of Gourock and Wemyss Bay had hitherto been worked by tender engines, some 4-4-0, some 4-6-0, and a number with large-wheeled 0-6-0s. But tank engines were ideal for these relatively short runs, and from their introduction the Pickersgill 4-6-2 tank engines had a virtual monopoly of the Gourock and Wemyss Bay services, until they were superseded, in L.M.S. days, by very efficient Fowler 2-6-4 tanks (reference 175). But the Pickersgill machines were strong, free-steaming engines, and a very useful task was found for them in banking duties at Beattock. The great majority of trains, passenger and goods alike, needed rear-end banking assistance over the very severe 10-mile bank between Beattock station and the summit, where the gradient is about 1 in 75 for most of the distance. On this duty some of the Pickersgill 4-6-2 tanks survived into the era of nationalization, and having borne the emblems and liveries of both the Caledonian and the L.M.S. they eventually carried the name BRITISH RAILWAYS on their side tanks.

85 **Robinson's 4-6-2 passenger tank;** Great Central Railway.
Reference has already been made (reference 59) to the work of J. G. Robinson on the Great Central Railway. The 4-6-2 tank engine illustrated is a very neat and handsome example of that engineer's designing skill applied to a powerful unit for fast suburban service. The first of the class, No. 165, was completed at Gorton Works at the end of 1910, and was, by a very short lead, the first of this wheel arrangement to be used in Britain. This Great Central example was followed very shortly by 4-6-2 tank engines on the London Brighton and South Coast Railway, and on the London and North Western (reference 69). The G.C.R. engines were designed for working from the London end of the line. One could hardly describe their work as suburban, because the first stations out of Marylebone were at Wembley Hill, on the Wycombe route, and at Harrow on the main line via Aylesbury. Their work thus consisted in a fast initial run through the immediate suburban area, with speeds of 60 m.p.h. or more, and then hard work in climbing the heavy gradients through the Chiltern hills. On some stopping trains, originally, they worked as far north as Leicester. On these duties, with an excellent boiler and relatively small coupled wheels, they proved a great success, and they worked on the residential services from Marylebone for nearly 40 years. After grouping, when engines of greater power were needed for the Tees-side services this Great Central design was chosen by the L.N.E.R. for further multiplication in preference to an existing North Eastern design.

86 **Reid 4-4-2 tank engine;** North British Railway.
The last of this group of passenger tank engines, the North British, dates from 1915, and was a superheated version of an earlier variety. The lines over which these engines were required to work were severely graded but, as in the case of express-passenger locomotives, W. P. Reid preferred four-coupled, to six-coupled wheels, and these 4-4-2 tank engines certainly did some good work. They were used on the longer distance residential trains from Edinburgh, working to Galashiels, both via Peebles and via the main line of the Waverley Route, over Falahill summit. Like all the North British designs they were massively built, and in consequence they were very low in maintenance charges, and had a long life. After larger and more modern engines had been put on to the fast suburban services around Edinburgh and Glasgow the Reid 4-4-2 tanks were usefully employed on lighter duties in Fife, on the Clyde Coast, and on certain workings

that took them up the West Highland line as far as Ardlui. The entire stud of North British 4-4-2 tank locomotives – the original non-superheated batch of 30, introduced in 1911, and the 21 superheated engines put to work from 1915 onwards – all survived to enter national ownership, in 1948, and it was not until the dieselization programme got under way from 1955 onwards that they were withdrawn.

87–89 **Dynamometer Cars;** Great Western Railway; North Eastern Railway; London and North Western Railway.
The accurate measurement of the performance of locomotives is an essential part of the science of railway engineering; but on many railways in pre-grouping days the size of the locomotive stud and the nature of the work involved did not justify the expense of constructing a dynamometer car, or of maintaining the necessary technical staff to man it, and to assess results. In pre-grouping days four companies owned dynamometer cars, and three of these are illustrated in our coloured pictures. Before mentioning the cars of the G.W.R., of the N.E.R., and of the L.N.W.R. individually, some reference is needed to the function of these cars. The basic function in all cases is to measure the work done by the locomotive, and this is first of all registered by a powerful spring, in exactly the same way as an ordinary spring balance works. The dynamometer, however, not only registers the pull at any moment, but in combination with an instrument called an integrator it clocks up the total amount of work done on the journey. The performance of the locomotive is recorded on a continuous chart passing through the integrator, registering also the speed at any moment. Automatically there are records produced on the chart which show speed, drawbar pull, total work up to the particular moment, while observers in the dynamometer car note the time of passing each milepost, important stations and junctions, and other incidents of the journey. An engineer is always riding in the cab of the locomotive, and he communicates by telephone details of the engine working, such as the extent to which the regulator is open, steam pressure, position of reversing gear, and so on. All these are noted down at the appropriate moment on the chart passing through the integrator, so that on completion there is a continuous record of the performance of the locomotive.

The Great Western car (reference 87) was built in 1903, and was used in recording the performance of the new standard range of locomotives Churchward was designing. In heavy express passenger work it was desired to have engines capable of sustaining a drawbar pull of 2 tons at 70 m.p.h., and the dynamometer duly recorded that the 'Saint' and 'Star' engines could do that. In 1924 the same car was used for the trials of the 'Castle' class 4-6-0 No. 4074 *Caldicot Castle*, and when the results were published the performance of that engine was so efficient so far as fuel consumption was concerned that engineers of other railways just could not believe it. The car was used extensively in the Interchange Trials of 1948, after nationalization, when locomotives of the Southern, Eastern and London Midland Regions were tested between Paddington and Plymouth; but one of the mightiest exhibitions of power output that this car was ever called upon to record was in 1953, when the ex-G.W.R. 4-6-0 No. 6001 King Edward VII was set to haul a train of *twenty-five coaches*, at normal express train speed, and this tremendous load of 800 tons was run for long stretches of the line at 65 to 70 m.p.h.

The North Eastern car (reference 88), shown in L.N.E.R. livery, was in many ways a copy of the Great Western vehicle. Wilson Worsdell, when Chief Mechanical Engineer, had borrowed the latter car, and then proceeded to build one of his own. The car shown in our picture recorded some famous occasions in locomotive history, such as the trials in 1923 between Great Northern and North Eastern 'Pacifics', and the high-speed running of the early streamlined 'A4' engines. But the greatest occasion in its career came in July 1938 when it was coupled next to the engine on the test train when the Gresley 'A4' Pacific No. 4468 *Mallard* made the world's record speed with steam traction. The instruments in the dynamometer car recorded the very thrilling speed of 126 m.p.h.

The London and North Western car (reference 89) was built in 1908, to replace the curious little six-wheeled car used by F. W. Webb. The handsome car shown in our picture was commissioned in time to record the magnificent performance of Bowen-Cooke's first superheater express locomotive, the *George the Fifth*, in 1910, and in 1913 it was used in the trials of the 'Claughton' class 4-6-0 No. 1159 *Ralph Brocklebank*, when some maximum output trials were conducted first between Euston and Crewe, and then between Crewe and Carlisle. On that occasion the values of horsepower registered were the highest that had been noted up to that time with any class of British locomotive. The maximum effort was one of 2¾ tons at 69 m.p.h. with an indicated horsepower of 1669. Thus each of these pre-1914 dynamometer cars had their great moments. After grouping the L.M.S.R. used the Lancashire and Yorkshire car in preference to that of the North Western.

90 **Dynamometer Car No. 3;** London Midland and Scottish Railway.

The science of locomotive testing had notably advanced in the years between the two world wars, and just before nationalization of the railways in 1948, the L.M.S.R. had completed an entirely new dynamometer car embodying the latest practices, and arranged for a novel new form of electrical control in testing. One of the advantages claimed for a stationary testing plant is that the speed of a locomotive can be kept constant. To work in conjunction with the new dynamometer car two mobile test units were designed, which with electrical controls could keep the speed of a locomotive constant, whether it was running uphill or down. The loading was entirely electrical, so that with the dynamometer car and two mobile test units, the effect of any weight of train encountered in ordinary service could be simulated. It sometimes caused astonishment to onlookers to see a powerful locomotive working very hard, hauling no more than three coaches, and possibly not exceeding 40 m.p.h. When maximum output trials were made of certain British Railways locomotives, as a counterpart to the 25-coach trials made with the G.W.R. 'King' class engine, the running characteristics of 850 and even 900-ton passenger trains were simulated without having to haul an inordinate number of coaches. Over the Settle and Carlisle line a 'Britannia' class 4-6-2 successfully hauled an equivalent load of 850 tons up the 14 miles of 1 in 100 gradient between Settle Junction and Blea Moor, while the Stanier 'Pacific' engine No. 46225 *Duchess of Gloucester* made equally good time with an equivalent load of 900 tons. The latter was without much doubt the greatest task ever set to a British express-passenger locomotive, and it was duly recorded in the dynamometer car shown in our picture.

91 **London and South Western Railway coat of arms.**

The South Western device is unusual in that it included five quarterings. This may seem a contradiction in terms, since a thing divided into five could hardly be considered to consist of 'quarterings'. But in writing of heraldry one uses heraldic terms, and the South Western device had two quarterings on the left hand, or dexter side, and three quarterings on the right, or sinister side. Originally there were only four quarterings, covering the extent of the London and Southampton Railway as originally built: London and Southampton, on the dexter side, Winchester and Portsmouth on the sinister. Later, when the first westward extension was constructed in the form of the branch from Eastleigh to Salisbury, the arms of the City of Salisbury were added – a simple device consisting only of eight bars alternately gold and blue. In later years the London and South Western Railway extended far beyond the territory indicated by the five towns on its coat of arms. Bournemouth, Weymouth, Yeovil, Exeter, Barnstaple, Plymouth, and Padstow were all served by fast express trains from London; but the coat of arms was not changed again, after the first amendment that took in Salisbury. On the timetables right down to the years just before the grouping the oldest form of the coat of arms was used, omitting Salisbury. The one shown in our picture was used on the Drummond locomotives, carried on the driving-wheel splasher. In the last locomotive built for the L.S.W.R. just before grouping the splashers were so small that the coat of arms could not be used.

92 **South Eastern Railway coat of arms.**
This line and its great rival, the London Chatham and Dover, were very much intertwined in the county of Kent. Most towns were served by both companies, and there was a great deal of overlapping and uneconomic working, so that amalgamation, or a fusion of interests was the inevitable outcome. But both the South Eastern and the London Chatham and Dover were concerns of great individuality, and the former in its coat of arms had a most beautiful design. It was rare, in not following the pattern of so many railway heraldic devices, but was a wholly original design. The centre-piece is the White Horse of Kent displayed on a red cross. This might have been intended as the emblem of the City of London; but the familiar dagger has been omitted, and it could have signified the St. George's Cross, of England. Above the cross, and still within the shield, are to be seen a demi-lion and a demi-ship. These items were taken from the coat of arms of the Cinque Ports, all of which were served by the South Eastern Railway. The heraldic design is completed by the crest surmounting the shield, which is a pleasant allusion to Dover Castle – Dover being the first terminus of the line. As can be seen from our picture, the colouring was magnificent, and the ensemble, encircled by the familiar garter, included the motto of the Company – 'Onward'. There were times during the nineteenth century, when passengers by the railway must have felt that the motto had more than a slightly cynical ring; but there were no half measures about the enterprise displayed, during the years of fusion with the 'Chatham'.

93 **London Chatham and Dover Railway coat of arms.**
The 'Chatham', as it was popularly known had a very chequered career in its early days, and the audacity with which it entered London and opened a series of highly competitive services with the slenderest of financial backing is one of the most fascinating and exciting stories of mid-Victorian railway history. But however daring, unconventional and provocative its early policies may have been, in its heraldry it displayed great dignity and beauty of design. The garter encircles four shields, and in depicting the final version in our picture it is interesting to recall an earlier one, in which London was not so much as included. The railway had its origin in the country, and made its way to London later, and the shields first included within the garter

were those of the county of Kent, and of Rochester, Canterbury and Faversham. The device illustrated has at the top the White Horse of Kent, and then from left to right, the City of London, the City of Rochester, and on the right, Dover. Although Chatham figured so prominently in the railway name the arms of the town were not displayed. Those responsible evidently thought that the ancient city of Rochester, so relatively near, was more appropriate than the dockyard town. The 'Chatham' also included a motto on their coat of arms 'Invicta' – always associated with Kent. The arms of the London Chatham and Dover Railway can still be seen, magnificently displayed on the piers at each end of the railway viaduct adjacent to Blackfriars Bridge, in London. The viaduct carries the busy line leading to St. Paul's and Holborn Viaduct stations.

94 **London Brighton and South Coast Railway coat of arms.**
This magnificent device was used rather sparingly on locomotives and coaching stock of the L.B. & S.C.R., and took two different forms. There was one in which the central shield was simply enclosed in a garter, and the more elaborate one shown in our picture, in which the shield had as supporters a griffin on each side, the wing of a griffin as the crest, and the Company's name on a ribbon below. This elaborate version was used on a few specially selected locomotives, and on certain saloon carriages. The towns included in the shield are top left, London; top right, Brighton; bottom left, and bottom right, Portsmouth. The town shields of Brighton and Hastings are in themselves of particular interest. Brighton itself is represented by the two dolphins on the shield within the shield, and the surrounding piece including the six martlet birds was added when Brighton was made a county borough, in 1897. The martlets formed the coat of arms of one of the oldest Sussex families – that of Radynden – through whose land the railway passed. The arms of Hastings are rather complicated heraldically, and are connected with the position of Hastings as the Premier Port of the Cinque Ports Confederation. Many other towns of importance were served by the L.B.&S.C.R., but in addition to London and Brighton, those of Hastings and Portsmouth were obviously chosen as representing the most easterly and westerly points reached by the railway.

95 **Travelling Post Office van;** Highland Railway.
The inception of the travelling post-office service has been described under reference 57, and before the end of the nineteenth century all the major railways, and some of the minor ones were running special vans for postal traffic. The Highland services were operated both north and south of Inverness, and the apparatus for picking-up and setting-down mail bags without stopping was in use at nearly all intermediate stations along the line. A characteristic of all T.P.O. vans is the gangway connection at the ends set to one side, instead of centrally on the coach. The T.P.O. vans are not connected to the ordinary passenger-carrying part of the train, and the offset gangway is to clear the sorting bench that extends from end to end of the vehicle. If it were not for the off-set the bench would have to be cut short, or tapered off at the ends to allow men to pass freely from one vehicle to another. The Highland van illustrated is one of three that have a very interesting history. During the first World War, when the Grand Fleet was based at Scapa Flow in the Orkneys, a huge volume of letters for the men passed over the Highland Railway, and the relatively small T.P.O. vans that had sufficed for the normal peacetime mail were quite inadequate. So three new vans were built at Lochgorm Works, Inverness,

embodying the characteristic narrow side-panelling, and the handsome, though very simple style of lettering and finish. These three vans had a long and strenuous life. They ran continuously on the Highland mail trains for 45 years, and were withdrawn at the end of 1961.

96 **Combined passenger coach, and travelling post office;** Great Western Railway.

In recent years the mail-train services on British Railways have come very prominently into the public eye through the dastardly attack and robbery that took place on the West Coast 'Up Special' some years ago; and in recent times generally attempts have been sustained to segregate mail from ordinary traffic on those trains that convey travelling post offices. It is all the more interesting therefore to study the picturesque Great Western clerestory roofed vehicle of Victorian times that includes a post office and passenger accommodation in the same coach body. The three third-class compartments at the left-hand end are non-corridor, and the gangway at the right-hand end in the picture is of the offset type for connecting to other postal vehicles that might be marshalled in the train. One can imagine that this hybrid form of construction was adopted for reasons of coach standardization. The Post Office would have specified the size of compartment they required for letter-sorting and other work, and this would not have required more than a six-wheeled coach, of similar length to the Great Northern T.P.O. van (reference 108). But rather than build a special length of frame and body the Great Western used their standard dimensions, and took advantage of the spare space that would have been available to put in these passenger-carrying compartments, and reduce the dead weight of the rest of the train by avoiding the use of extra carriages.

97 **Tri-composite corridor brake coach;** South Eastern and Chatham Railway.

For all its own services, including the most luxurious of the Continental boat trains, the South Eastern and Chatham used only non-corridor carriages. But in the early 1900s, the enterprising management concluded arrangements with both the London and North Western and with the Midland Railways to run through-carriages from the Kent Coast resorts to certain northern cities. These coaches were worked to Willesden Junction in the one case, and to Kentish Town in the other, and there attached to expresses from London to the Midlands and the North. These involved long journeys, such as to Leeds or Manchester; and so that passengers in the through S.E.&C.R. coaches could enjoy the amenities of long-distance travel, such as restaurant cars, special corridor carriages were constructed. They included first-, second- and third-class compartments, and a commodious luggage compartment. This had also the picturesque and characteristic S.E.&C.R. 'birdcage' roof, whereby the guard could look out over the roofs of the ordinary carriages. It made an interesting sight to see one of these vehicles, in the rich lake colour of the S.E.&C.R. marshalled next to the engine on a London and North Western express. Equally strange was it to see on the Midland Railway a vehicle providing second-class accommodation. The Midland was the first railway to dispense entirely with second class. This bold move took place as long previously as 1875. Ordinarily one could not buy a second-class ticket on the Midland; but obviously some special arrangement must have been made for the running of those S.E.&C.R. through-carriages, because second-class accommodation was available in them throughout from Leeds, or Manchester to Dover! On the L.N.W.R. there would be no difficulty, as that company was still booking all three classes in the early 1900s.

98 **Tri-composite lavatory carriage;** Cambrian Railways.
The headquarters of this otherwise very Welsh railway was in England, at Oswestry, Salop. This was not only the administrative centre of the Cambrian, but also the site of the locomotive and carriage works. At the turn of the century the engineer in charge of these works as Locomotive, Carriage and Wagon Superintendent was Mr. Herbert E. Jones. All his training and early engineering experience had been on the Midland, and he had served under such outstanding railwaymen as Matthew Kirtley, S. W. Johnson, and that most distinguished of nineteenth-century carriage designers, T. G. Clayton. This goes some way towards explaining the remarkably comprehensive and enterprising work carried out in the shops at Oswestry. There, not only were locomotives maintained, and repaired, but new construction was undertaken from 1901 onwards; and some fine examples of contemporary coaching stock were also built in this relatively small works. In actual style the coaches of the Cambrian Railways may not have been very outstanding; but the livery was most distinctive, and their riding qualities excellent. The Cambrian participated in the working of many through-carriage services with the London and North Western Railway, and though such vehicles were not required to run fast on the parent system, they were taken along pretty smartly once they passed off Cambrian metals at Whitchurch. The roof boards on these through-carriages were evidently designed to have a keen advertising value, as for example when one saw a six-wheeler prominently labelled thus: CAMBRIAN RAILWAYS THROUGH CARRIAGE BETWEEN LIVERPOOL (Lime Street) AND ABERDOVEY TOWYN AND BARMOUTH VIA CREWE AND WHITCHURCH. There were no abbreviations to shorten the legend – not even an St. for Street, and no short cuts by use of the ampersand. In later years the Cambrian, like the Brighton, the Furness, and other users of two-tone colour schemes, abandoned the white upper panels, and painted its coaches green, though still handsomely lined out.

99 **'Experiment' class 4-6-0;** London and North Western Railway.
After George Whale had succeeded F. W. Webb as Chief Mechanical Engineer of the L.N.W.R. in 1903, a complete modernization of the motive power was undertaken, and following the great success of the 'Precursor' class 4-4-0s in the Southern Division an adaptation of the same general design to suit the Northern Division was prepared. To provide greater adhesion, for coping with the steeply graded line through the Westmorland fell country, six-coupled wheels were used, instead of four, and this involved an important change in the design of the firebox. At first the men found some difficulty in mastering the technique of firing this shallow grate, and the engines got an indifferent reputation. Some doubts were also spread in certain quarters by the choice of name for the class. The first engine took both name and number from the first Webb three-cylinder compound, which certainly *was* an experiment. Whale's 4-6-0 of 1905 was equally not one, and when the men had mastered the art of firing, the engines did good work. Eventually no fewer than 105 of them were built at Crewe works, and although the increasing loads of the Scotch expresses led to their early replacement on the mountain section they put in many years of useful service in general passenger work all over the L.N.W.R. system. They were very fast runners, and several instances of speeds

in excess of 90 m.p.h. have been recorded with them.

100 **57-ft. Corridor composite carriage;** London and North Western Railway.

At the same time as modernization of the locomotive stock of the L.N.W.R. was in progress at Crewe, the carriage works at Wolverton was engaged in the production of some fine new rolling stock. The carriages of the North Western, and of the West Coast Joint Stock had always been renowned for their comfort and smooth riding; but with the exception of the beautiful twelve-wheeled dining cars the carriages had been rather narrow, and with relatively low ceilings inside. The production of the so-called '57-ft. stock' was a major advance, and it included spacious new carriages for the 'set' trains on the Liverpool and Manchester, and the Anglo-Scottish services, and the production of new self-contained composite carriages with luggage compartments, for use on services where a single through-carriage was run from destinations off the principal express routes. Until the grouping, in 1923, a single coach was all that was generally needed for the day service between Birmingham and the Scottish cities, and a 'brake-composite' labelled BIRMINGHAM NEW STREET AND GLASGOW CENTRAL was attached at Crewe to the front of the 10 a.m. express from Euston to Glasgow. When originally built the North Western was still booking second-class passengers on its internal services, and some of these composite carriages provided accommodation for all three classes.

101 **A 'Barochan' class 4-6-0;** Caledonian Railway.

Caledonian locomotive practice had some points of similarity to that of the L.N.W.R. in the use of medium-powered 4-6-0 locomotives on many passenger trains, although the Caledonian used a few very large engines on the Anglo-Scottish services, over Beattock summit. The engine illustrated was one of an important intermediate class, with coupled wheels, 5 ft. 9 in. diameter, against the 6 ft. 6 in. of the largest passenger engines. They were used on the north line from Glasgow Buchanan Street to Perth, where there are heavy gradients, and little chance of really fast running, and they were also used on some of the highly competitive services from Glasgow to Gourock, where the combination of train and boat used to involve all-out races from Glasgow across the Firth of Clyde to Dunoon. Again there were certain hindrances on the run down from Glasgow at junctions where speed had to be reduced. In consequence an engine with a capacity for rapid acceleration was essential in order to keep the sharp times required by the timetable. The *Barochan* was named after the residence of Sir Charles Renshaw, the Chairman of the Caledonian Railway, whereas the ever-famous main-line express engine *Cardean* was named after the estate of the deputy-Chairman. One might have imagined that the names would have been reversed, but the *Barochan* was used on Clyde Coast trains between Glasgow and Gourock, and daily passed near to Sir Charles Renshaw's home.

102 **A 'Grampian' corridor carriage;** Caledonian Railway.

In the early years of the present century the intense rivalry between the East and West Coast routes from London to Scotland which had reached a climax in the great Race to the North in 1895 had largely subsided south of the Border; but in Scotland the North British and the Caledonian were engaged in severe competition for the traffic from Glasgow and Edinburgh to Aberdeen. Not only were some very fast services introduced, but both companies built some luxurious new rolling stock for the principal trains. The Caledonian named its 10 a.m. express out of Glasgow the 'Grampian', although curiously enough its route to Perth and Aberdeen did not pass through the Grampians and gave its passengers no more than a distant sight of some of the eastern outliers of the range. Whether the name was strictly appropriate or not the rolling stock put on to that train was magnificent. All the coaches were mounted on twelve-wheeled bogies, and they rode superbly, although speeds were, by the very nature of the route, not exceptionally high. Some similar coaches, slightly shorter and on eight-wheeled bogies, were built for general service, and one of them was used on the through-carriage service between Glasgow and Bristol via the Severn Tunnel route. Two of these beautiful carriages have been preserved, and are restored to the original Caledonian livery as shown in our picture.

103–106 **Semaphore Signals.**
There was no more picturesque feature of the British steam railways than the semaphore signal. Through by far the greater part of the steam era signals of the lower quadrant type were used, and in general terms the indications displayed were widely known: Horizontal, with a red light at night, meant STOP, and an arm inclined downwards, with a green light at night, means ALL RIGHT, or PROCEED. What is not so generally appreciated however is the remarkable variation in detail that existed between the semaphore signals of the different railway companies. There were important differences in signalling practice – all, of course, within the code of safety working which was so cherished a tradition of all the individual railway companies – but in these first four examples I am concerned with differences in details of construction. To the casual observer a 'semaphore signal' was just a signal, all looking very much alike; but a connoisseur, on coming upon a line of railway would be able to identify the owning company beyond any doubt from the form of the signals, before any train, or any other sign of ownership was sighted.

The Great Eastern semaphore (reference 103)
As in the great majority of semaphore designs the arm itself was made of wood tapering in width from 11 in. at the top to 10 in. at the centre point of the pivot. Naturally a wooden blade of this kind, after years of service, tends to split, and one would often see metal bands put on to check this tendency. But the Great Eastern put these bands on when the signals were new. The arm pivot and spectacle was of an interesting design in cast iron, and the spectacle glasses were of a rather complicated shape that would have needed some careful cutting. The actual colour of the 'green' glass needs some further comment. Originally these glasses were of a very beautiful grass-green colour; but with an oil-lighted lamp behind them, and a flame having a strong yellowish colour, the result at night was a rather pale yellow-green. To counteract this, in later years the glasses were made of a strong blue-green colour – in fact some looked decidedly more blue than green. In combination with the yellow light from the oil lamp a much more distinctive green was displayed at night.

The Caledonian semaphore (reference 104)
The signals of this railway were immediately distinctive in being carried on posts of open wrought-iron lattice work, instead of the more usual wood. The iron 'flats' forming the lattice were turned on edge, as seen from the front, and this earned for the particular form of construction the term 'inconspicuous lattice', as distinct from the 'conspicuous' lattice used on some posts on the Great Northern

Railway (see reference 191). Apart from the post itself, however, the Caledonian design of semaphore was distinctive in the method of attachment of the spectacle casting to the pivot plate. All the bolt holes were slotted, so that the position of the spectacle could be adjusted, within certain limits in respect to the centre of the post. So far as can be traced the Caledonian was the only railway to use this form of construction, which was adopted so as to facilitate the sighting of signals on curves where it might be necessary to set the line of the light beam slightly oblique to the line of the railway at the particular point where the signal itself was mounted. The Caledonian always retained the grass-green spectacle glasses, and until quite recent years one could see the pale yellow indication at night.

The North Eastern semaphore (reference 105)
As mentioned in describing the early primitive forms of semaphore (reference 51–52), the original method was to have the arm working in a slot in the post. The type of mounting was retained to the very end of lower quadrant semaphore signalling on the North Eastern Railway. The principle of working in a slot in the post was, indeed, used even when certain lattice post signals were installed; and to carry it out a somewhat complicated form of construction was necessary, in order to provide the necessary mounting in the middle of the lattice. On a wooden post, as shown in our picture, the cutting away of the centre of the mast to accommodate the arm and its bearings naturally weakened the post, and to compensate for this reinforcing strips were added on each side for the length of the slot. Another very characteristic feature of North Eastern signals was the pinnacle, which was no less than 4 ft. high! Actually this was a design used in many parts of the world by the famous firm of signalling contractors McKenzie and Holland Ltd. of Worcester. The base and the ornamental fluted portion was of cast iron and the spire was made in sheet zinc, wrapped round, and secured to the topmost flange of the casting.

The Great Northern semaphore (reference 106)
This design, which originated after the disaster at Abbots Ripton in 1876, was intended to provide against the risk of an arm becoming weighted down by snow, and accordingly giving a false indication. It was pivoted at the centre of the arm, and was designed to assume a vertical position, when in the clear. In actual practice the arms rarely came off to the truly vertical position. It was more usual to see them as in the illustration of the Great Northern gantry (reference 191). This design was taken up by McKenzie and Holland Ltd. as one of their standard products, and it was adopted by the local railways in South Wales, and also on certain railways in Australia. It provided a splendidly distinctive day indication, and naturally made any line belonging to the Great Northern instantly distinguishable. Our picture shows one of these centre-balanced arms – sometimes referred to as 'somersault' signals – mounted on a wooden post, though in later years it was more normal to mount them on lattice-iron posts of the 'conspicuous' type.

One feature that will be noticed in comparing these four examples of lower quadrant signals, is that while the form of the arm – a red blade with a white band – is standard, the proportions of the red and white portions vary considerably. There was certainly no uniformity between the various railway companies in this respect.

107 **Ocean Mail stowage van;** Great Western Railway.
The conveyance of mail by railway has

led to the construction of many distinctive and extremely interesting vehicles, and two of these have already been noticed under references 95 and 96. For the Ocean Mail traffic from Plymouth to London the Great Western built some huge 68-ft. stowage vans, with sliding doors, and high elliptical roofs, in complete contrast to the clerestory-roofed vehicles that had been standard on the G.W.R. from quite early broad gauge days. These vans were completed in 1904 in time to be used on the very fast runs made in the spring of that year when competition with the London and South Western Railway was at its height. Some similar vans were included in the new all-Postal train to the West of England put into service in 1905, though this train included a number of older vehicles with clerestory roofs. This mixed formation on the West of England postal special persisted for more than 20 years. The record-breaking mail train of May 9, 1904, when the 4-4-0 locomotive *City of Truro* attained a maximum speed of 100 m.p.h. descending Wellington bank, consisted of four of the big 68-ft. stowage vans and one older vehicle. This latter was detached at Bristol, and the load with which the Dean 4-2-2 engine *Duke of Connaught* completed the 118 miles from Bristol to Paddington in the amazing time – for the year 1904 – of 99¾ minutes, was four of the stowage vans, a total of 120 tons.

108 **Six-wheeled Travelling Post Office;** Great Northern Railway.

The network of postal services conveyed by railway reached its maximum in the years just prior and after the first World War, before the rapid development of motor transport on the roads. There were three main postal routes for long-distance traffic, and many others were feeders or subsidiaries. Strange though it may seem, at first sight the principal route from London to the North East coast was from Euston, and not from King's Cross, using the trains to be mentioned under references 109 and 110; but the Great Northern Railway had a number of post office contracts for both day and night services to districts lying short of the main arteries of North Country postal services, and for these some travelling post office vans were constructed. In the early years of the present century the apparatus for picking-up and dropping mail bags at speed was very extensively used, and there were postal nets at many stations along the routes. The local postmen used to clear these nets, and delivery of the mail was within quite a limited area. Nowadays the 'apparatus' as it is known in the postal service is used to no more than a limited extent, and loading and unloading of mails is largely confined to the stations at which the mail trains stop. The Great Northern T.P.O. van illustrated is typical of the six-wheeled era, though the coachwork and the finish, in varnished teak, was as fine as anything put into the most palatial corridor carriages or dining cars of a later time.

109 **T.P.O. van for the Postal Special';** West Coast Joint Stock.

In ordinary railway parlance a 'special' is an extra train: something outside the ordinary timetable. In the Post Office, however, the DOWN SPECIAL and the UP SPECIAL are the regular Anglo-Scottish postal trains which convey no passengers, except on the final section of the Aberdeen run, north of Perth in each direction. It was the UP SPECIAL that was concerned in the great mail robbery when the train was so audaciously held up near Leighton Buzzard. The DOWN SPECIAL in steam days usually left Euston with 12 vehicles. Some of these were stowage vans for through traffic, but a number of them contained the 'apparatus', and even today mails are exchanged at quite a number of places en-route. Mails for North-Eastern England are conveyed by this train as far as Tamworth, where they are transferred to the Midland train (reference 110) and there is a general exchange of mails during the stop at Crewe. The mail-exchanging apparatus is fixed only on one side of the carriage and the sorting bench extends the full length of the carriage on the opposite side. The lineside nets are, of course, be mounted on the left-hand side of the line, looking in the direction of running, and because of this the train has to be turned end for end before commencing the return journey so as to have the apparatus on the correct side for the nets. At the London end the train is turned on the Mitre Bridge triangle at Willesden. Our picture shows one of the vans built specially for the service by the L.N.W.R. at Wolverton Works.

110 **Six-wheeled Travelling Post Office van;** Midland Railway.
The Midland and the North Eastern Railways combined to operate the second important trunk route of railway postal service in this country, operating between Bristol and Newcastle, and intersecting and connecting with the West Coast 'Specials' at Tamworth. The route of the 'Midland T.P.O.' as it is identified on postmarks of letters posted on it is via Gloucester, Birmingham, Derby, Sheffield, and York, and thus connects with many centres of population and industry. Subsidiary services feed into it at Bristol and Cheltenham, and it receives a heavy mail from the south at Tamworth, where special arrangements are in force for rapid transhipment of mailbags between the high-level Midland platforms, and the low-level North Western below. The Midland van illustrated is an early clerestory-roofed vehicle of Clayton's design, with the simple lettering 'M.R.'; but the bogie T.P.O. vans used on this service at a later period bore the initials 'M.&N.E.J.P.S. – Midland and North Eastern Joint Postal Service. Whether in Midland or North Eastern territory, however, the postmark in recent years has always been 'Midland T.P.O. Going North' or 'Midland T.P.O. Going South' as the case might be. Our picture shows clearly the offset gangway, and the ventilators for the gas lamps that provided the internal illumination. In later years, with electric lighting, additional lights were mounted low down on the bodies outside for the benefit of men working the 'apparatus'.

111 **Robinson's standard 0-6-0 goods engine;** Great Central Railway.
Following the construction of the London Extension line, in 1899, and the tremendous drive for new traffic that followed J. G. Robinson embarked upon the building of a new standard range of locomotives that would anticipate the needs of the traffic; and at the same time as he introduced the 4-4-0 express-passenger class, reference 59, he built a generally similar 0-6-0 for general goods service, as illustrated in this picture. Rarely can there have been a neater, or more handsome 'common hack' freight engine. They were nicknamed the 'Pom-poms', and although superseded later by the much larger and heavier eight-coupled engines introduced by Mr. Robinson their general usefulness continued without any break. On four occasions the greatest possible tribute was paid by other railway authorities to the locomotive designs of J. G. Robinson. First, during World War I, his 2-8-0 was chosen by the Ministry of Munitions as a standard for working on the military railways behind the Western Front. Then, after grouping, two of Robinson's designs – the 4-6-2 passenger tank, and 4-4-0 'Director' class – were chosen for further construction by the L.N.E.R. Lastly, and perhaps most remarkable of all, in 1945, when Sir Nigel Gresley's successor, Edward Thompson, was drawing up a schedule of standard locomotives for the

future requirements of the L.N.E.R. the 40-year-old Great Central 'Pom-pom' was chosen to be the future standard medium-powered goods and branch-line engine. Unfortunately for the memory of the Great Central Railway nationalization supervened, and no further engines of this class were constructed; but in 1945 there were 174 of them at work.

112 **Composite slip-brake carriage;** Great Central Railway.
Under reference 60 one of the early carriages built for the London Extension services was illustrated, in the very handsome colours then adopted. In later years a reversion was made to the varnished teak style of the old Manchester Sheffield and Lincolnshire Railway, and the accompanying picture shows a clerestory-roofed carriage of this later period. The Great Central made very extensive use of slip carriages, for giving fast services to intermediate points without stopping the main train. One of the most remarkable was that of the so-called 'Sheffield Special', which, in fierce competition with the Midland, ran non-stop from Marylebone to Sheffield, not calling even at Leicester or Nottingham. A slip-coach was detached at Leicester, covering the 103 miles from London in 105 minutes. The Great Central, like the great majority of railways using slip coaches, did not provide gangway connections to the rest of the train, so that the 'slip' itself had to be self-contained with first- and third-class compartments, lavatories, luggage space, and compartments for the slip guard at either end. An interesting example of multiple slip-coach working was to be seen on Great Central line right down to the year 1936, on the 6.20 p.m. express from Marylebone. The train ran non-stop to Leicester, but carried two slip coaches, the first detached at Finmere, whence it was conveyed forward to serve the intermediate stations of Brackley, Helmdon and Culworth, and the second at Woodford. In those later years, however, the slip coaches were of Mr. Robinson's massive elliptical-roofed later design, similar in general appearance to the coach reference 132; but the service remained the same.

113 **Bogie third-class carriage;** London Brighton and South Coast Railway.
The Brighton has sometimes been referred to as little more than a suburban railway, and now, with almost the entire mileage of the old L.B.&S.C.R. electrified on the third-rail system the vision of the management of some 60 years ago has come true. So far as train services are concerned, it is almost as convenient for a London business man to live at Brighton, as in an outer residential district of London. In these days of extreme road congestion he probably gets home quicker! Even back at the turn of the century the Brighton was a short distance main line and there was no thought of introducing corridor stock. The type of coach illustrated was in regular use up to the time of grouping, and thereafter until new stock was put on by the Southern Railway. It is true that on some later trains newer coaches with high elliptical roofs were put on. But these, too, were non-corridor. Our picture shows the two-tone colour scheme in use in the early 1900s. Memories of these coaches extends as much to the insides as to the exteriors. While most other railways decorated the interiors with attractive pictures of places served by the railway, and both the Great Western and the Midland used the beautiful photochrome prints of the period, the Brighton filled the space over the headrests with snappy advertisements. One that I always remember ran thus:

'When nights were bold
They all wore armour;
Nights hot or cold
Wear Swan's pyjamas!'

Not living anywhere on the Brighton line I never discovered what Swan's pyjamas were like; but such is the value of advertising, in that the amusing piece of doggerel so sticks in the memory.

114 **Billinton's 2-6-0 express goods engine;** London Brighton and South Coast Railway.

Although the Brighton Railway was above all a passenger line, there was a considerable freight traffic to and from the Continent via the Newhaven–Dieppe route. In Victorian times the celebrated superintendent William Stroudley had produced his famous small-wheeled 0-4-2 type of locomotive for the 'Grand Vitesse' continental goods service, and Billinton was following in the same tradition in 1913 when he built the first example of the 'K' class 2-6-0 for the continental traffic. At that time the 2-6-0 was coming rapidly into favour as a standard type for mixed traffic, and its success on the Great Northern and Great Western undoubtedly prompted this interesting Brighton development. Five of the 'K' class were built in 1913–14; but due to the heavy increase in traffic by the Newhaven route during the war, five further engines of the class were built in 1916. The Brighton Works had a long and cherished tradition of excellent workmanship and massive construction, and these 2-6-0s were ideal for the fast and heavy goods trains. After the war some further engines were built at Brighton, but the grouping of the railways in 1923 resulted in no further construction of them once that batch was completed. Nevertheless, they were long-lived engines, and 'saw steam out' on the continental freight workings.

115 **Rebuilt non-superheater 4-4-0;** Midland Railway.

In the early years of the present century R. M. Deeley, who succeeded S. W. Johnson as Locomotive Superintendent of the Midland Railway, commenced a large programme of locomotive modernization, part of which consisted of the rebuilding of many of the older 4-4-0 locomotives with large boilers. Johnson had made something of a point in having small boilers, as a means of ensuring that the engines were worked 'on a light rein' as it were, and thus with maximum economy. Deeley's reboilering, though still using saturated steam, increased the nominal capacity of the engines, though this programme of renewal was accompanied by a general re-organization of the locomotive department which fixed rigid limits for train loading. These rebuilt 4-4-0s, which were placed in No. 2 class, were limited to a maximum load of 180 tons, and a great deal of double-heading was required as a consequence. Nevertheless these rebuilt engines filled a useful gap between the passing of the Victorian era, of very small engines, on the Midland, and the era of superheater engines – albeit still of small proportions – as inaugurated by Sir Henry Fowler. The re-organization of the locomotive department was accompanied by a complete re-numbering of the stock. The small raised brass figures on the cab sides previously used were replaced by large transfer numerals on the tender, while at the same time the style of lining-out was made less ornate. But the turnout of individual engines remained as always on the Midland, immaculate.

116 **David Bain's design of 'brake-first';** Midland Railway.

In 1902 there began a change in carriage design on the Midland that coincided roughly in time with the modernization of the locomotive stud. Bain, who succeeded T. G. Clayton in that year, came from the North Eastern Railway, and while he followed the handsome profile of Clayton's later clerestory carriages he came to abandon the rectangular panelling, and windows with top lights, in place of a more conventional appearance. Furthermore, the vogue of large numerals, evident on the engine tenders, also spread to the carriages, which had large figures '1' and '3' on the doors, instead of the full word 'first' and 'third'. The Bain carriages were magnificently finished both inside and out. The upholstery in both first- and third-class compartments were the finest of the day, and the exterior finish included no fewer than *seventeen* coats of paint. The ordinary carriages, as distinct from the dining and sleeping cars, were lit by compressed oil gas, and this was unfortunately the cause of two not very serious collisions becoming major disasters, through the igniting of the gas and many coaches being burnt out. Notwithstanding the tragedies of the Hawes Junction and Aisgill disasters, in 1910, and 1913 respectively, the Midland clerestory carriages both of Clayton and Bain are remembered with admiration by those who had to make long journeys in them. Our picture shows a purely Midland vehicle, as used on London–Leeds, London–Manchester and Bristol–Leeds expresses. Similar coaches were provided for the Scotch services worked jointly with the North British and with the Glasgow and South Western Railways. These carriages were lettered 'M.&N.B.' and 'M.&G.S.W.' respectively.

117 **Worsdell's 'V' class Atlantic;** North Eastern Railway.
The early years of the twentieth century, if not a time for any great competition in speed between the various British railways, was a time for competition in passenger amenities and in the building of very large and imposing locomotives. In retrospect one queries if such great machines were really necessary at that time; but whether necessary or not, the North Eastern Railway was certainly in the forefront of the movement, and the magnificent-looking 'Atlantic' engine shown in our picture could scarcely be bettered on the score of fine appearance. It was built at Gateshead in 1903 and was the forerunner of a class of hard-working, heavy weight-pulling machines, that had a life of more than 40 years. The inspiration for the adoption of the 'Atlantic' type was said to have come from a visit of North Eastern Railway officers to America, where they were able to witness the good work being done on the Philadelphia and Reading Railroad. But there is another story of their introduction that is amusing. When Wilson Worsdell returned from his visit to America his Chief Draughtsman, Mr. W. M. Smith, was ill. Now Smith was a most forceful personality, as well as a very sound engineer, and when he was restored to health, and returned to his office the story goes that he was extremely annoyed that the big new 'Atlantic' had been designed in his absence and orders given for its construction. Wilson Worsdell had a very difficult hour, listening to all the reasons why the engine should not be built. But events had progressed too far for any alteration to be made, and eventually the 'V' class engines proved to be good, hard-working machines, though somewhat heavy on coal.

118 **Elliptical-roofed corridor carriage;** North Eastern Railway.
In referring to the later Midland Railway coaching stock (reference 116) mention was made that David Bain had previously been Carriage Superintendent of the North Eastern Railway. In his time the coaching stock was mainly with clerestory roofs: a square type, as used on the Great Western, and in Clayton's earlier work on the Midland Railway, for non-corridor coaches, and an ornate bow-ended design on those coaches that were built by the North Eastern Railway for the East Coast Joint Stock. During the early years of the twentieth century Mr. H. N. Gresley, as he then was, developed an entirely new style of carriage roof on

the Great Northern Railway, using a high elliptical shape, and at the same time an elegantly curved bow-end. Carriages of this design were built for the London–Newcastle services operated jointly by the Great Northern and the North Eastern Railways, and lettered 'G.N.&N.E.'. The Gresley style influenced carriage design on the North Eastern itself, and the coach illustrated is one of a series built for the North Eastern Scotch services between Leeds and Glasgow. This provided a fast morning connection to Edinburgh and Glasgow, with connections at Edinburgh for Aberdeen and Inverness, and the fine stock run in these trains was always very much admired. Similar coaches were used on the Newcastle–Liverpool expresses run jointly with the Lancashire and Yorkshire Railway. In this case the stock was provided in equal numbers by both companies, each running complete trains.

119–124 **Subsidiary Semaphore Signals.**

The signals previously described and illustrated under references 103 to 106 are what are termed 'running' signals. They were used to control movements from one signal to the next, and if encountered in the danger (horizontal) position compelled a stop. In the vicinity of stations, however, many shunting and subsidiary movements are required, and where it was necessary to authorize a driver to proceed for a limited and clearly defined distance within the station or yard limits, or to back, small subsidiary semaphores were mounted on the same posts as the running signals, and below them, to authorize some restricted movement beyond a running signal that would be in the danger position. The form of such subsidiary signals was not governed by any national code of aspects. In most cases they were designed to suit the conditions existing on individual railways and as can be seen from the illustrations (references 119 to 124) they exhibited some striking differences, though not all these signals had the same function. In general the idea was to have some signals that would be not only much smaller than the standard semaphore, but quite unlike it in form, so that there would be no chance of confusion. In later years, also, some endeavour was made to avoid using red lights as the stop indication of these subsidiaries, so that when a running movement was signalled and the main arm was cleared the driver did not have to pass a red light, albeit a very small one.

Great Western Railway (reference 119)
This little arm certainly passed the test for distinctiveness from the main-line running signal. The striping was horizontal instead of vertical, and it authorized a shunt ahead, for a limited distance beyond the running signal which would be mounted on the same post. In certain localities notice boards were erected at the side of the line displaying the words LIMIT OF SHUNT.

London and South Western Railway (reference 120)
This semaphore performed the same function as that of the Great Western Railway (reference 119), and the diamond-shaped plate made it instantly distinguishable from the ordinary running signals. The London and South Western Railway also used the form of subsidiary arm shown in reference 121, for what is referred to as a 'calling on' movement, and in this respect the usage was similar on the Great Eastern Railway, which is the actual design illustrated, and also on the Highland Railway.

Great Eastern Railway (reference 121)
The function of a 'calling on' signal may best be explained by an actual instance of operation. As its name suggests, it was used to 'call on' a train, at very slow

speed, into a section that was already occupied. One could imagine a long platform being no more than partly occupied by a train, while another one was waiting at the entrance. Under strict working rules the signal at the entrance to the platform would be kept at danger, because the line between that signal, and the next one at the exit from the platform was occupied. But having stopped the second train at the entrance, time would be saved by 'calling it on', at dead slow speed into the platform, up to the limit that the line was unoccupied, so that loading, and unloading could proceed. The 'calling on' signal had in its turn to be distinctive in shape from a 'shunt' signal, because the former gave authority to proceed as far as the line was unoccupied – often until the engine of the second train almost touched buffers with the last coach of the first one – whereas the shunt signal only authorized a movement up to a certain place on the line.

Midland Railway (reference 122)
This shunt signal was, except for one detail, a miniature edition of the ordinary running signal, even to the distinctive Midland shape of the spectacle plate, and the form of the stop, that prevented the arm rising to any extent above the horizontal position. The only distinctive feature was the 'T' portion on the end, which certainly showed well on these little arms in the day time.

London Brighton and South Coast Railway (reference 123)
The use of ringed arms varied considerably on different railways, but it was certainly an excellent way of providing a distinguishable mark for a subsidiary signal. A very interesting feature of this Brighton signal is that no indication at all was provided at night when the arm was in the 'on' position. The red light of the main signal was evidently considered sufficient, without there being a subsidiary red light. When the arm was lowered the white light of the oil lamp became visible, and thus there was no possible chance of any confusion with the red and green lights of the main signal.

Great Western Railway (reference 124)
This company used quite a variety of subsidiary arms, and the one illustrated in this picture was termed a 'backing' arm. It was often to be seen at the *entering* end of a station platform, facing the opposite way to the main direction of traffic. At many stations it was necessary to attach or detach vans, or small coaches, and the backing arm would be used to signal away a station pilot engine that had been used for marshalling work, or to signal the driver of a train to set his whole train back from the platform into a siding for traffic purposes.

The six examples of subsidiary signals selected for illustration are only a very few out of a great variety of types that were used on railways in the pre-grouping era. They are nevertheless sufficient to indicate the ingenuity and care taken in the steam era to safeguard and expedite the working of the traffic.

125 **The Taff Vale Railway coat of arms.**
This amazing little railway, which had such a traffic in coal that it took some 270 locomotives to work 112 miles of line (!!) originally had a coat of arms enclosing the feathers and motto of the Prince of Wales in a circlet; but this was later abandoned in favour of the remarkable affair illustrated in our picture. A humorous description of it written in 1921 by the great locomotive historian E. L. Ahrons cannot be bettered: 'There are some large railway companies in this country whose coats-of-arms are too involved to attract attention, and, on the other hand, there are other designs which one notices at once. Amongst the latter is the familiar London & North

Western's Britannia. But the Taff Vale picture puts even Britannia completely in the shade, and is evidently emblematic of the whole of Wales, though the Taff Vale occupies only a very small corner of that country. It must be the goat that does it. He is perched on the top, evidently monarch of all he surveys, and you cannot miss him, even if you try. I like that goat. I have seen him marching at the head of a famous Welsh regiment with the same air of proud defiance that he shows on the Taff Vale carriages. But the animal which accompanies the goat, placed within an oval scroll beneath him, is by no means so majestic. At first glance he looks like a screaming eagle of the American pattern, but a closer examination shows him to be intended for something else. Some years after my first acquaintance with him, I learnt that, in addition to the goat, Wales claims a heraldic dragon, and I suppose, though I am open to correction, that the Taff Vale coat of arms endeavours to depict that animal, though I hope that the real Welsh dragon is of more respectable appearance. The Taff Vale variety – genus *Draco Tonypandiensis* – is a dancing, shrieking, riotous beast, engaged in putting out his tongue at the goat and doing his utmost to disturb the stately serenity of the latter. He would even shake up a Chinaman who is popularly supposed to know something of the habits of his kind.' The whole thing is tremendous, and is fitly concluded by the unpronouncable motto beneath: *Cymru a fu Cymru a fydd*, which means 'Wales hath been and Wales shall be'.

126 **Rhymney Railway coat of arms.** The Rhymney was the near neighbour and close rival of the Taff Vale in conveying coal from the mountain valleys to the Cardiff Docks for shipment, literally to all parts of the world. The pronunciation, by the way, is 'Rumney'. Great foreign railways like the Paris, Lyons and Mediterranean sent their own colliers to Cardiff to fetch the choice Welsh coals, and the Rhymney Railway on its coat of arms symbolized the great business activities of the region rather than the flamboyant national sentiments emblazoned on that of the Taff Vale. But that was typical of the intense rivalries of the railways in the valleys. It was not so much a rivalry for traffic in the boom years, for there was so much coal produced that the extreme congestion nearly brought both railways to a standstill, and the coal owners promoted yet another line to tap both the Rhondda and the Rhymney valleys, and take a proportion of the coal to a new port at Barry. The Rhymney Railway coat of arms embodied a curiosity in that it included, bottom right, the arms of Newport, which it never served. The other shield is that of the City of Cardiff. Above is a picturesque drawing of an Egyptian furnace, as introduced at Rhymney Iron Works in 1828, while the inclusion of a ship emphasizes the great importance of the export trade in coal. Altogether this was a very interesting and colourful coat of arms.

127 **Cambrian Railways coat of arms.** The name of the interesting system was always used in the plural, so much so that on wagons which were not large enough for the full name, it was abbreviated to CAM.RLYS. The Cambrian, in geographical extent was much the largest independent railway in Wales, though, of course, its traffic was not to be compared with the prodigious carriers of coal in the mining valleys. The Cambrian was rather a line of mid-Wales, though curiously enough its headquarters, and locomotive and carriage works were in England, at Oswestry, Shropshire. The Cambrian was a main line, and it had several important through connections with both the Great Western and with the London and North Western. With the latter

company its principal connection was at Whitechurch, on the Shrewsbury-Crewe line, and over this route through-express services were run between Aberystwyth and Manchester. There were two different colour schemes in its coat of arms. The one included in our picture was that used on locomotives, with the central shield divided between the dragon of Wales and the rose of England. On the handsome green carriages, one of which is shown in reference 98, the background to the shield was black and the dragon and rose were on a background of orange and deep purple respectively. The surrounding garter had orange letters and cords, and above, left and right on the black ground to the shield were the letters 'C', 'R' and 'Co'.

128 **Festiniog Railway coat of arms.**
It is no exaggeration to write that this little narrow gauge line in North Wales has a history not only without parallel in its vicissitudes and fascinating interest; but it is a history with a significance out of all proportion to the size and traffic of the railway itself. The coat of arms now carried on locomotives and carriages includes the insignia and motto of the Prince of Wales, just as the locomotives of the Cambrian Railways carried that same insignia on their tenders. Nevertheless, while the Festiniog Railway continues to be a living symbol of Welsh enterprise and is a first-class tourist attraction today, its original purpose was the conveyance of slates, and out of the problems arising from the phenomenal growth of that traffic came the development of the articulated Fairlie double-engine, two examples of which are still at work on the line. It was on the Festiniog that the potentialities of the articulated principle were so vividly demonstrated, and although subsequent development took ways other than the original Fairlie design, the seeds were sown on the Festiniog, and the development many years later, in the form of the Beyer-Garratt, proved to be one of the finest products of the great British export trade in steam locomotives. If ever the Festiniog Railway Company should consider adopting a different or a more elaborate coat of arms, I would suggest that slates and the articulated locomotive should find a part in it.

129 **Ocean special saloon;** Great Western Railway.
In years between the two world wars the attention of the Great Western Railway upon the ocean traffic at Plymouth took a new form. Whereas in the early 1900s it was a case of making record times with the mails, and beating the London and South Western, at the later period, when Southampton had become the terminus station of Cunard and White Star liners, the Great Western was strongly advocating the calling of eastbound liners at Plymouth to save English passengers the time spent in what was otherwise the normal procedure, namely of making the first European call at Cherbourg, and then crossing to Southampton. By calling at Plymouth a full day was saved on the journey from New York to London. Everything possible was done to make things attractive on the railway journey. The Ocean Specials were given preferential treatment on the line, and the coaching stock provided was of the very finest. In addition to ordinary vehicles a small number of special saloons were built with particularly luxurious accommodation, and each named after a member of the Royal Family. These coaches were built out to the maximum width permitted by the generous Great Western loading gauge – no less than 9 ft. 7 in. in overall width. They were, without much doubt, the finest vehicles available to ordinary passengers that have run on the railways of this country.

130 **David Bain's Royal Saloon;** Midland Railway.

Unlike the railways over which frequent Royal journeys were made, such as the London and North Western, and the Great Western, the Midland did not maintain a full Royal train; but the very fine vehicle illustrated in our picture was built in 1912 for inclusion with other vehicles if a special should at times be required. It was purely for day use, and internally contained a main saloon with a smoking-room and a ladies retiring-room at either end. Presumably one did not smoke in the main saloon! Although not built until 1912 its interior decoration contained all the rich ornamentation and upholstery characteristics of the Edwardian era. Royal journeys on the Midland Railway may not have been very frequent but, as can well be imagined, when the opportunity came the Company did things in style. The saloon would be marshalled in a train of David Bain's finest clerestory carriages, finished as only Derby could finish coaches in those spacious days when even the ordinary 'thirds' had seventeen coats of paint. The engine used also had special treatment. It was not enough to select a specially good one and burnish it to the last degree. For the occasion it became completely anonymous. The large number on the tender was painted out, and instead of the beautiful Midland coat of arms on the cab sides (see reference 24) the Royal Cipher and crown was substituted.

131 **Saloon Carriage No. 1;** Furness Railway.

Although it was no more than a local line, the Furness Railway had a reputation of doing things in good style, and the handsome saloon shown in our picture is a good example. In its early days the railway had its rather primitive coaching stock finished in a nondescript style of varnished wood, without any lining, as illustrated in Sir James Ramsden's inspection car (reference 10). But as the railway got into its stride and began to develop that high sense of publicity and purpose that came hand in hand with the vast development of the traffic centred upon Barrow, the old style of coach painting was changed for the distinctive two-tone royal blue and white shown in the picture. This harmonized remarkably well with the engines in iron-ore red. In the ordinary way Furness carriages did not work far beyond the confines of their own system. The through services to other parts were usually worked by 'foreign' carriages, London and North Western for Euston, and Midland to Leeds and St. Pancras. But the Furness carriages, quite apart from the vehicles like special saloons, were very good and would have been an excellent advertisement for the company wherever they went. In World War I the two-tone colour scheme was abandoned, and the coaches painted royal blue over-all, though retaining their gold lining, and the Company's beautiful coat of arms, see reference 175.

132 **Open Saloon 'third';** Great Central Railway.

In its period of development, following the completion of the London Extension in 1899, the Great Central was using every known device to attract more traffic, and much was being done to advertise the attractions of what was then still a new route, by the running of attractive and extraordinarily cheap excursions. One of the most remarkable was an Easter excursion from Manchester to Plymouth, worked throughout by a Great Central engine. In 1910 under the direction of Mr. J. G. Robinson some fine new saloon carriages were built specially for the excursion traffic, at Dukinfield Works. These had doors only at the ends, and a characteristic feature, not at all usual then in British practice, was the use of large, deep windows each covering one section of the car. The interior was divided equally into smoking and non-smoking sections, and each had seats for 32 passengers, with 8 tables for four at each side of the centre gangway. The idea of providing tables opposite every seat was an extension of the rather exclusive dining car idea of the Midland and of the Great Northern in which dining passengers were a race apart, as it were. But on the Great Central here was the same principle applied to very cheap fare excursion travel. Externally the coaches were attractively finished with narrow vertical panelling in varnished teak, and the coach bodies built out to the maximum permitted by the loading gauge.

133 **Corridor third-class carriages;** Great Eastern Railway.
The enterprise of the Great Eastern Railway in the early years of the twentieth century knew no bounds. Before the end of the Victorian era, although the lengths of run were short compared with those of the great trunk lines to the north and west of England, the Great Eastern had introduced restaurant cars on the Cromer expresses, though at first unconnected with the rest of the train. But full corridor trains soon followed and the Company reached the height of its holiday traffic prestige in the working of the celebrated Norfolk Coast Express which ran non-stop over the 130¼ miles from Liverpool Street to North Walsham. This was a train solely for the Norfolk Coast. Large centres like Colchester, Ipswich and even Norwich were passed without stopping. The minimum load of the train was one of 12 coaches, of which 8 went to Cromer, 2 to Sheringham, and 2 to Mundesley. The coach illustrated formed part of the very fine and uniformly styled trains of 1907, and was used in the summer service each year from July to September. During the winter months there was not so great a demand for bulk travel from London to the Norfolk coast. There were times, of course, when extra vehicles had to be added to the regular set, sometimes at the last minute, and then it was not always possible to preserve the fine uniformity of the train. Older coaches, sometimes even six-wheelers were used for 're-inforcing' – as the railway operating term goes. But uniformity or not, the Norfolk Coast Express was an outstanding railway operating achievement.

134 **Twelve-wheeled dining car;** Midland joint Scotch stock.
The Midland Railway, unlike its rivals on the East Coast and West Coast routes to Scotland, had to feed two entirely different routes north of Carlisle, in providing through-trains to Edinburgh and to Glasgow. It is true that both East Coast and West Coast routes served both Scottish cities as well; but their operating arrangements were simpler. Trains for both Edinburgh and Glasgow, by West Coast took the Caledonian route out of Carlisle, and the bifurcation did not take place till Carstairs. On the East Coast route, one travelled through Edinburgh to reach Glasgow. On the Midland route, for many of the services, separate trains for Edinburgh and Glasgow were run throughout from London, each having their own restaurant car, or sleeping cars in the case of night journeys. In the early days of Clayton's very fine bogie coaches it was difficult, at a first glance, to distinguish the dining cars from ordinary vehicles, as both had the small windows traditional from the earliest days. But on the great majority of Midland trains, Anglo-Scottish or otherwise, the dining cars were the only vehicles in the trains to carry roof-boards. Our picture shows a typical dining car of the period before 1890, when Clayton had temporarily abandoned the clerestory roof. The car is one allocated to the joint service with the Glasgow and South Western Railway, and is labelled 'London St. Pancras and Glasgow St. Enoch'.

135 **Non-corridor bogie composite carriage;** Somerset and Dorset Joint Railway.

The picture to which this note refers has been chosen not so much to represent the Somerset and Dorset Joint Railway, as to be typical of the ordinary English railway carriage of the early Edwardian era. It is relatively simple and unpretentious in appearance, yet designed to provide comfort and space, if not the height of luxury in both first- and third-class compartments. It made tolerable the jog-trot of the ordinary through-trains between Bath and Bournemouth, and being non-corridor it provided more seating per unit of dead weight than would have been possible in a corridor vehicle and any reduction in dead weight was worth having on a line so severely graded as the Somerset and Dorset. In exterior design, if not in its livery, the coach bears a strong resemblance to the standard non-corridor coaches of the London and South Western Railway. This was no coincidence; for while the Midland Railway, as one of the two joint owners provided the locomotives, the South Western was responsible for the coaches, other than the corridor coaches of the Midland line which worked through to Bournemouth from the north. Though they were no more than local train stock these Somerset and Dorset non-corridors were beautifully finished externally with full lining-out, and the Company's coat of arms twice on each side.

136 **Open 'brake-third' corridor carriage;** Lancashire and Yorkshire Railway.

Much of the intense passenger business of the Lancashire and Yorkshire Railway was of a short distance nature. The policy of the Company was to run relatively short trains, and many of them. The express trains were sharply timed between the many intermediate stops, and on the purely Lancashire and Yorkshire service between Liverpool, Manchester, Bradford and Leeds, the 'set' trains consisted of only 3 coaches. But the L.&Y.R. combined with the North Eastern to run an excellent dining train between Liverpool and Newcastle, for which the two companies provided a six-coach corridor train on alternate days. I may add that the North Eastern operated a similar service with the rival of the L.&Y.R. – also serving Manchester and Liverpool, with a through dining-car train from Newcastle. This, of course, was over the London and North Western route and served Leeds and Huddersfield intermediately, while the L.&Y.R. served Wakefield. Our picture shows one of the fine carriages built for the L.&Y.R. Liverpool – Newcastle service. The complete train, which included separate dining cars for first- and third-class passengers, accommodated 51 first and 226 third class. It was a very popular service, and frequently loaded almost to full capacity. In Lancashire particularly there was a great affection for the 'Lanky', as the line was popularly called. The local people felt it was their own railway, managed by local men, and they preferred it to the London and North Western, which some people felt was too big and widespread a concern to give proper attention to the particular needs of Lancashire. The status of the L.&Y.R. was nevertheless a national rather than a local one, and when the two companies amalgamated in 1921, it is significant that some of the most important posts in the new combine went to 'Lanky' men.

137 **Churchward's 'County' class 4-4-0;** Great Western Railway.

It was in 1901 that G. J. Churchward drew up his celebrated plan for the complete standardization of the locomotive stock of the G.W.R. The main-line engines were to consist of no more than six classes, all with two outside cylinders, and inside Stephenson link motion. The 'County' class 4-4-0 of 1904 was one of these standard designs. It was built to work over those sections of the line where 4-6-0s were precluded from running because of weight restrictions; but these 4-4-0 engines were also on main routes for which 4-6-0s could not be spared, on account of more arduous duties elsewhere. In consequence the 'Counties' were to be seen on the West to North route from Bristol to Shrewsbury via the Severn Tunnel; on the Bristol and Birmingham route via Cheltenham and Stratford-on-Avon, and on the main line to Worcester via Oxford. They were fast and efficient engines, though somewhat rough riding; and although they had relatively small boilers they steamed well, and did excellent work on the heavy gradients of the line through the Welsh border country. Their names covered all the counties served by the Great Western Railway in England and Wales, and also many counties in the south and west of Ireland which were reached by the Great Southern and Western Railway working in connection with Irish boat service via Fishguard and Rosslare.

138 **70-ft. Corridor carriage;** Great Western Railway.
In his great programme of rolling-stock modernization Churchward not only aimed to build more powerful and more efficient locomotives but designed carriages that should have a minimum of dead weight for the number of passengers carried. The Dean clerestory carriages were excellent examples of design for their day, and the all-third coaches weighed 24 tons, while providing seating for 54 passengers. In his new 70-ft. coaches of the early 1900s, Churchward provided seating for 80 passengers, in coaches having a tare weight of only 33 tons. The ratio of dead weight to number of passengers seated was reduced even though the new carriages were considerably more spacious and generally more modern in their design. The first examples were painted in the traditional G.W.R. chocolate and cream livery; but as a measure of economy this was soon changed to all brown, and then to the handsome lake colour shown in our picture, which remained the Great Western standard until 1923. One drawback to the use of such lengthy carriages was that they could not be used on certain routes where the structural clearances were below those of lines at one time laid on the broad gauge. They could not be used on the West to North expresses, either by the Severn Tunnel route or on that via Stratford-on-Avon. A minor restriction in the West of England also prevented their being used on the Ilfracombe branch.

139 **Hawksworth's 'County' class 4-6-0 of 1945;** Great Western Railway.
The 'County' class engine of 1945 was the final development of the classic Churchward two-cylinder locomotive, with inside Stephenson link motion. It included a number of features pointing towards the future development of Swindon locomotive practice, particularly in its use of the very high boiler pressure, with a copper firebox, of 280 lb. per sq. in. This second 'County' class on the G.W.R. was, like the first one, built against restrictions in weight. It was originally hoped to use the same boiler as that on the 'Castle' class, but the weight came out too heavy, and the boiler used was to a new design. The locomotives were built just at the end of World War II when materials were in short supply, and it was difficult to get new tooling done. Because of this it was found convenient to use the flanging blocks that had been made during the war when Swindon Works were building, by Government order, Stanier 2-8-0 goods engines of the L.M.S. type. The 'Counties' were fast and powerful

engines, but their development was not fully completed by the time the railways were nationalized. Then other policies were adopted on a national scale. The 'Counties' did well on the heavy gradients of the Cornish main line, and especially so on the steeply graded route of the north main line between Wolverhampton and Chester. In all 30 were built and their names were taken from English and Welsh counties. There were no Irish names in the Hawksworth series.

140 **Bow-ended corridor carriage of 1947;** Great Western Railway.
When F. W. Hawksworth succeeded C. B. Collett as Chief Mechanical Engineer of the G.W.R. in 1941, it was soon clear that while many old Swindon traditions would continue in others changes could be expected. After the end of the war an entirely new style in main-line carriage stock was evolved. The Churchward practice of using 70-ft. coaches for heavy main-line working wherever possible had largely disappeared before the war, and after the special 'Centenary Riviera' coaches of 1935 (reference 158) a style very similar to that currently in vogue on the L.M.S.R. was adopted, with steel panelling, and large deep windows. After the war Hawksworth developed this style, but introduced the bow-ended roofs that had been so marked a characteristic of Great Northern and L.N.E.R. practice. The new coaches, which were not restricted by length in their sphere of operation, were thus a blend of L.M.S.R. and L.N.E.R. practice, while retaining the beautiful chocolate and cream livery of the Great Western. Their introduction was to a large extent piecemeal and there were no new dining cars to match. Luxuries had to give way to necessities in those years of austerity. Trains like the Cornish Riviera Express continued to be a mixture of old and new stock, and it was not until the Bristolian express was restored to its full pre-war speed in 1954 that a complete seven-coach train of the Hawksworth carriages was seen in regular operation.

141–144 **Distant Signal Arms.**
The function of a 'distant' signal in semaphore days was to provide drivers with ample warning that they were approaching a signal at which a dead stop might be required. As the stopping distance from a speed of 60 to 70 m.p.h. might be more than half-a-mile these 'distant' signals had to be located some distance before the 'stop' signals and some method of distinguishing them from signals at which a stop was compulsory was desirable. Until the 1920–30 decade the danger position of both distant and stop arms was indicated by a red light at night, though the arms themselves were distinguished by a fish-tailed end. Later, an amber light became the standard night indication of a distant signal in the caution position. Prior to that, one of the few attempts to distinguish home and distant signals at night was the Coligny-Welch illuminated indicator placed alongside the lamp as shown in our picture of a London-Brighton and South Coast distant signal arm (reference 141). At that time the painting of the arm was the same as for a stop signal, namely red and white, though the white band took the form of a chevron, in conformity with the shape of the end of the arm. In localities where track alignment, or other local conditions made it undesirable to indicate the existence of a clear road through the station ahead by exhibiting a distant arm in the clear position, 'fixed' distant signals were used, and an example of this, on the London and North Western Railway is shown in our picture (reference 143). This signified a permanent state of caution over the line ahead. This illustration also shows the distinctive L.N.W.R. type of semaphore arm which unlike most of its contemporaries was a steel pressing, with longitudinal corrugations to give stiffness.

These arms were made in the locomotive works at Crewe. Reference 142 shows the earlier form of distant arm used on the Midland Railway, when the front face of the blade was painted red, with a white disc, and the back was white with a black horizontal stripe from end to end. The back of the blade was divided equally into three sections painted white, black and white respectively. Of these different versions of the distant signal arm the last (reference 144) shows the final design used on the Great Western Railway, when amber had been standardized as the night indication of the 'caution' aspect. At the same time, distinction in the day-time indication was made, not only in the use of the fishtail end to the arm but by painting the blade yellow, with a black chevron. The latest Great Western semaphore arms were made from steel pressings, but of a considerably simpler design than that of the London and North Western Railway. Stiffness was achieved by means of a simple flanging of the edges, keeping the face of the blade completely flat.

145 **Tall Semaphore Signals;** Great Western Railway.
This illustration provides an interesting case where two pairs of semaphore arms are used on the same post co-acting with one another. A description of the actual location will make it clear why this form of construction was adopted. The line is on a slight left-hand curve, and the speed of express trains was high. To give long-sighting over the top of the station buildings the main arms had to be fixed high; but as such they would have been almost impossible to see from the guard's stance when giving the 'right-away' to a stopping train from the rear end of the platform. Co-acting arms were therefore necessary; but owing to local conditions and considerations of the sighting from the footplate the signal post had to be placed as close as possible to the track. A special design of arm was used, in which nothing projected beyond the right-hand side of the post. This design of co-acting arm, in a main running signal, is a greatly enlarged version of the mechanism used in the shunt arm (reference 119), though in this case with standard painting. This form of arm, which was used in a number of localities where clearances were limited, enabled the post to be located a good 12 in. nearer to the running lines than would otherwise have been the case. The co-acting arm was identical in size and painting to the standard 4-ft. running arm, while in the assembly shown in reference 145, the arms at the top of the post were the standard 5-ft. arms.

146 **Tall Semaphore Signals;** London and North Western Railway.
The need to provide the earliest 'advanced information' of the state of the line ahead was well recognized on all railways where the schedules demanded fast running, and the London and North Western Railway more perhaps than any other administration carried this principle to an extreme extent in providing signals of exceptional height, that could be seen from long distances away against a 'sky' background. Posts of 50 ft. and 60 ft. were common, and there were a few as high as 70 ft. In certain cases co-acting arms were used lower down the post, but the example shown in our picture is representative of standard practice on quadruple tracked sections of line. First of all, the signals relating to the fast and slow lines were distinguished by those of the latter being fitted with a ring. Some companies used ringed arms only for subsidiary purposes, and others, like the Great Western, used them only in sidings. But the North Western used them for running movements on the main line, where there were fast and slow lines alongside. Another characteristic of the

L.N.W.R. was to place all these tall signals at the left-hand side of the line. Thus between Roade and the approaches to London, a distance of nearly 60 miles, the signals for the up-fast line would have to be read across two intervening tracks, as the sequence of running lines on this section, from left to right seen from the engine was: 'Up Slow'; 'Down Slow'; 'Up Fast'; 'Down Fast'.

147 **Large-boilered 'Claughton' class locomotive;** London Midland and Scottish Railway.
When C. J. Bowen-Cooke was planning a 'super' express passenger engine for the London and North Western Railway, in 1910, by using four cylinders all driving on to one axle he hoped, by the elimination of all hammer-blow effect on the track, to be able to use a considerably heavier load per axle that had hitherto been permitted by the civil engineer. But Bowen-Cooke was in advance of his time, and it was dead weight and the effect of unbalancing that governed the civil engineer's judgment, and as originally built the 'Claughton' class engines had to have smaller boilers than were originally planned. In 1924, however, after Bowen-Cooke had died, and the L.N.W.R. had become part of the huge L.M.S.R. system, the work of the Bridge Stress Committee showed that the original contention had been correct. Locomotives that were scientifically balanced were allowed to have considerably greater axle loads than previously permitted, and a number of the 'Claughtons' were rebuilt with much larger boilers. The engines had then been displaced from the heaviest express duties by the new 'Royal Scot' class; but the rebuilt engines were used to great advantage on the Irish Mails, on the Manchester expresses working over the North Staffordshire line, and on the Liverpool and Manchester Scotch expresses between Preston and Carlisle. Engine No. 5986 shown in our picture was one of those stationed at Preston for the last-mentioned duty.

148 **Open-third saloon carriage;** London Midland and Scottish Railway.
In the last years of the Midland Railway, when David Bain had been succeeded by R. W. Reid, as Carriage and Wagon Superintendent, the long tradition of clerestory-roofed carriages was ended, and coaches generally similar to the final Bain design, but with high elliptical roofs were introduced on the principal express services. At the time of grouping R. W. Reid became Carriage and Wagon Superintendent of the L.M.S.R. and the Midland influence was naturally strongest in formulating the designs of new carriages. Except for dining cars, the Midland had previously used none save compartment stock – unlike the Great Northern and the Great Central which had included a number of open saloons in the make-up of many trains. But in the new era the L.M.S.R., while continuing to build compartment corridor stock, very similar in outward appearance – as well as in colour – to the final Midland designs, also introduced the open saloon type of carriage, with tables for four on each side of the gangway. These had the advantage that they could be used simply as saloons, but also as third-class dining cars. In some of the new trains used soon after the grouping an entirely separate eight-wheeled kitchen car was run, marshalled between the first- and the third-class dining car. On large and important trains, such as 'The Royal Scot' and 'The Merseyside Express', additional open-third saloons were included, apart from those reserved particularly for dining.

149 **Rebuilt 'Lord Nelson' class 4-6-0;** Southern Railway.
When O. V. S. Bulleid succeeded Maunsell as Chief Mechanical Engineer of the Southern Railway he made a number of

striking changes, both to the design and to the appearance of some of the existing locomotives. The 'Lord Nelson' class in its original form had been no more than partly successful. The boiler was not over-free in steaming, and the cylinder and valve design although permitting of very fast running on occasions, did not develop a very high output of power. Although no external change was apparent, the cylinders were completely redesigned; but the most striking external change was made to the chimney. Instead of the previous single blast-pipe of conventional design, Bulleid substituted the five-nozzle multiple blast-pipe designed by the French engineer Lemaitre, and this needed a chimney of much greater diameter. This change, combined with the redesign of the cylinders, put the 'Lord Nelson' class in the very front rank of British locomotive practice. Perhaps even more startling to the eye was the change in style of painting. In the place of the quiet, almost sombre, olive green of Maunsell's day Bulleid painted the Southern express locomotives in a vivid malachite green, which made them as spectacular to see as their performance became under his changes in technical detail.

150 **Standard corridor coach, Bulleid era;** Southern Railway.
Bulleid applied himself no less energetically to the matter of main-line carriage design on the Southern Railway. With the object of eliminating the cost of painting he made some experiments with plastic-sided luggage vans, and in an attempt to convey more passengers in the suburban rush hours he built for experiment some double-decker trains. Neither of these experiments was successful; but in the development of standard main-line corridor stock he built some fine new train sets for the Bournemouth service in 1947. These trains were built in six-coach sets, and it is the 'brake-third' of one of these sets that is illustrated in our picture. These trains were also finished in malachite green to match the locomotives; but quite apart from painting some interesting details of their construction may be noted. In the compartment stock in particular the slenderness of the side walls was evident, arising from the all-welded body framing, eliminating the need for heavy uprights, and the laying of plates, and so on, one above the other in building up. Externally the finish was completely smooth, and while lovers of the historic may perhaps regret the passing of the traditional form of carriage construction with stout timber bodies and elaborately lined panelling, as an expression of modern techniques the Bulleid carriages were very fine.

151–4 **Auto-trains.**
The problem of securing economic operation of country branch lines was receiving the attention of many railway managements in the early 1920s. Until that time the general practice had been to use small locomotives that had been displaced from more important duties, and to make up the branch trains from equally obsolescent rolling stock. The passengers had to put up with cramped and out-of-date carriages, and the locomotive working in many cases was neither smart nor efficient. Then there developed the idea of the self-contained auto-train, or steam rail motor cars, as they were sometimes called. Our pictures show some variations of this principle, which was to have a small steam locomotive of modern design and a coach mounted on the same frame, to work one unit. In some cases the engine was designed powerful enough to haul a trailer, if necessary. But in all cases a commodious carriage of modern design was provided, and the smart turnout make an attractive ensemble. The Furness Railway rail motor (reference 151) was typical of the type using a vertical boiler and a roomy driving cab

at the front of the unit. It was designed to haul a smart four-wheeled trailer, and curiously enough both motor coach and trailer were unusual in Furness Railway coaching stock practice in having clere-story roofs. It was used at various times on the short branches running from the main line into the heart of Lakeland, and was very popular in connection with the numerous circular tours by rail, coach and steamer organized by the Furness Railway. One of these branches ran from Ulverston to Lakeside station, at the foot of Windermere, and the second ran from Foxfield, up steep gradients to Coniston. These auto-trains looked very smart in the white and royal blue livery, though for reasons to be mentioned later they had a relatively short life. On the Great Northern Railway rail motors of a different type were constructed for light branch working. Our illustration shows a combined unit designed for the Edgware branch. Here again the loco-motive and carriage were mounted on a single frame, but the locomotive had a boiler of the orthodox type, and the driver and fireman worked from a nor-mal locomotive footplate, albeit rather a small and cramped one. The carriage was a large affair, built to main-line standards, and by painting the loco-motive green and finishing the coach in varnished teak, another very attractive-looking unit was produced, see reference 152. The Lancashire and Yorkshire Rail-way became quite an extensive user of rail motor cars and at one time no fewer than 18 of them were at work. They were introduced at various times between 1906 and 1911, and some of the engines lasted until 1948. These L.&Y.R. rail motors were more successful, and more long-lived than most of their contemporaries because the engines and carriages were readily detachable from the others, although coupled into a single unit for operating. The coach unit was mounted on an ordinary coach bogie at the rear end, and at the forward end it was secured to the engine by an extension girder. Engines and coach units could be interchanged and this eliminated the disadvantages of the single-unit type, like the Great Northern, in that an engine needing repair did not necessarily put the auto-train out of commission, as another engine unit was available to couple to the coach. For serving intermediate places, with the least possible expenditure on new equipment, a number of 'halts', without platforms were established, and to enable passengers to descend in com-fort, retractable steps were fitted on the coaches. As our picture (reference 153) shows, engines and coaches were painted in the standard Lancashire and York-shire style. Some rail motor cars intro-duced at about the same time had the engine units painted in the carriage colours. This was the case on the South Eastern and Chatham, and on the Glasgow and South Western Railways. The Great Western, as might be ex-pected from its multitude of country branch lines, was a very large user of steam rail motor cars, and by the year 1908 no fewer than 99 motor coaches, and many trailers, were at work. The standard types developed after early experiments were built externally in the style of the latest main-line corridor stock, in two lengths, 70 ft. and 59 ft. 6 in. Our picture shows a 70 ft. motor coach, to haul a 59 ft. 6 in. trailer. Internally, like all the rail motor cars illustrated under references 151–154, the coaches were of the open saloon type, one class only, but extremely comfortable. I have the most vivid recollection of these cars in their hey-day, because I frequently travelled on one working on the branch from Reading to Basingstoke as a very junior schoolboy returning from Reading West station to Mortimer. They worked all over the G.W.R. system, frequently being used to provide stopping trains, or feeder services, on the main lines, between the running of fast expresses. An interesting example was to be seen in the Chippenham and Bath districts in the 1920s. Rail motor cars were used on the Chippenham–Calne branch, and their workings were also dovetailed in with the main-line trains. For example the 4.15 p.m. Plymouth express from Paddington slipped a coach at Chippenham. This was then attached as trailer to a rail motor car, and the coach that had been hauled down from London at express speed was then taken forward to Bath behind a rail motor stopping at all stations, and providing an excellent fast service from London to roadside stations like Corsham, Box, and Bathampton. The over-riding disadvantage of the self-contained rail motor car like those used on the Great Western was that the slightest defect would put both an engine and a coach out of service, and for this reason the integrally mounted locomotives were removed, and small tank engines of standard design used to haul the trailer cars.

155 **The 'Maid of Morven' observation car;** Caledonian Railway.
It was not until comparatively recent years that the scenic beauties of some sections of the British railways were exploited for tourist traffic. The London and North Western and Cambrian Railways built observation cars for working on certain routes in North Wales, and the North British put saloon carriages with large windows on to the West Highland line. But one of the finest cars ever built specially for a scenic route was the Pullman observation car worked over the Caledonian line between Glasgow and Oban. The Pullman cars running in Scotland were used as restaurant cars on ordinary trains, rather than working in the English style as vehicles in which passengers travelled for the entire journey on payment of a small supplement. In Scotland they were operated on a number of Caledonian routes, and there was one over the Highland line between Perth and Aviemore. All these cars were named after ladies famous in Scottish history, such as Mary Seton and Flora Macdonald. The beautiful observation car working on the Oban line was named *Maid of Morven*, and as our picture shows it was remarkable for the huge curved windows at the rear, extending almost from floor to ceiling. It was a wonderful experience to traverse the full length of the Oban line in this car, and to watch the gradual passage of magnificent mountain scenery. Once the Highland proper was entered, at Callander, there was no fast running and the journey could be enjoyed at leisure.

156 **'Waverley route' sleeping car;** M.&N.B. Joint Scotch Stock.
The operation of the through-express service between London St. Pancras and Edinburgh Waverley dates from 1876, the year in which the famous Settle and Carlisle route was opened. At first the sleeping accommodation on the night trains was provided in American type Pullman cars, but in later years the 'Midland and North British' joint stock, lettered 'M.&N.B.' was of standard Midland design and built at Derby carriage works. These cars had the standard low clerestory roofs, and were uniform in profile with the beautiful carriages forming the rest of the trains. Prior to World War I there were two night trains in each direction between St. Pancras and Edinburgh, and for a short time after the war this lavish facility was restored. But after the formation of the L.M.S.R., the night service over the Waverley route, via Hawick and Galashiels, was reduced to one sleeping-car express in each direction. After grouping, when new sleeping cars were required for this service they were built at Wolverton, to

the latest London and North Western design as provided for the West Coast Joint Stock, and it is one of these cars that is shown in our picture. They were magnificently equipped and the external finish was, of course, in the standard L.M.S. style. It was nevertheless unusual to see a vehicle of L.N.W.R. design lettered 'M.&N.B.'.

157 **The Coronation Observation Car;** London and North Eastern Railway.
To mark the coronation of King George VI the L.N.E.R. put on a very fast afternoon service making the journey between London and Edinburgh in the unprecedented time of 6 hours, for the run of 392¾ miles. The streamlined 'A4' Pacific engines were used, as on the very successful Silver Jubilee service (references 159, 160), but Sir Nigel Gresley added to the Coronation trains the very distinctive 'beaver-tail' streamlined observation cars. The shape of these cars was not just a publicity 'stunt'; the form provided for a very smooth effect at the tail end, eliminating all the eddies and turbulence that exists in the immediate rear of a fast train. And the Coronation, like the Silver Jubilee did at times travel very fast indeed! On my first journey with the Coronation we attained a speed of 106 m.p.h. During the winter months the observation cars were not run, as almost the entire journey was made in darkness; but during the summer it was a delightful experience to ride in these cars, and to see all the incidentals of a busy railway journey receding rapidly from one's view. The coaches of the Coronation train were finished in two very pleasing shades of blue: Cambridge blue for the upper panels, and Garter blue for the bodies. The five locomotives originally allocated to the working of this train were also painted Garter blue, and this later became the standard colour for all the streamlined 'A4' Pacifics.

158 **'The Centenary Riviera' stock;** Great Western Railway.
In 1935 the Great Western Railway celebrated the hundredth anniversary of its incorporation. Because of the grouping of the railways in 1923, and of nationalization in 1948, no other railway in Great Britain will ever achieve the distinction of operating, under the same name, for 100 years or more. Naturally the event was made the occasion of many special celebrations. It was a time of steady evolution and a time when some old traditions were being discarded, and this trend was seen particularly in the new trains built at Swindon Works for the 'Cornish Riviera Express' service. The Great Western called itself 'The Holiday Line', and at that time there was a substantial all-the-year-round traffic to Devon and Cornwall. The 'Cornish Riviera Express' was unquestionably the 'flagship' of the passenger services of the Company, and the new carriages were of special design, built to the maximum width permitted by the loading gauge. On routes which had been 'broad gauge' in earlier days the loading gauge was more generous than elsewhere, and advantage was taken of this to provide carriages of exceptional width and comfort. Their use had to be restricted to routes where the loading gauge was wide, and on the sole bar there was a notice: NOT TO RUN OVER THE EASTERN OR WESTERN VALLEYS NORTH OF WOLVERHAMPTON OR BETWEEN LITTLE MILL JCT. AND MAINDEE JCT.

159–160 **Britain's first streamlined engine and train;** London and North Eastern Railway.
The introduction of the high-speed streamlined service between London and Newcastle in the autumn of 1935 was one of the truly outstanding events in British railway history. Sir Nigel Gresley was much interested in the working of the

two-car high-speed railcar service introduced in Germany between Berlin and Hamburg, and some consideration was given to a similar service between London and Newcastle. But it was found that a far better train, with the usual lavish passenger accommodation could be provided with ordinary steam locomotives than with diesel-electric railcars of German design. Some high-speed trial runs were made with standard Gresley 'Pacific' engines, and the decision was made to introduce a high-speed train of limited coach formation to provide a four-hour service between London and Newcastle. A study of L.N.E.R. 'Pacific' performance in relation to more recent practice both in Great Britain and abroad suggested that improvements in design could be made with advantage, particularly in view of the continuous running at speeds of 75 to 90 m.p.h. needed with the new train. Furthermore, having regard to the special nature of the service, and the publicity that would undoubtedly be attached to it, it was decided that the locomotives should be streamlined externally. It was the year of the Silver Jubilee of King George Vs reign, and the train itself was named 'The Silver Jubilee'. Also Sir Nigel Gresley decided that instead of finishing engine and train in the standard L.N.E.R. colours – attractive and traditional though they were – the whole train, engines and coaches alike would be 'silver', with the coaches having stainless steel lettering on the sides. The combined effect of the streamlined exterior and the unusual painting was startling and from its first appearance the class 'A4' Pacific caught popular fancy to an extent unparalleled by any other new locomotive. It provided the silver streamlined link between London and Newcastle, and so 'Silver Link' the first engine was named. Four engines of the class were built, and the others were *Quicksilver*, *Silver King* and *Silver Fox*. If the appearance of the engine was startling, even more so was its performance. On its trial run it attained a maximum speed of 112½ m.p.h., and showed it could climb the long gradients on the route at a steady speed of 80 m.p.h. This was perhaps more important than the very high maximum, because it meant that a steady, uniformly-high speed could be maintained throughout. The original train consisted of 7 coaches, all of which included the principle of articulation, which Sir Nigel Gresley had very successfully used in his standard main-line corridor stock and dining cars. For example the dining cars of 'The Silver Jubilee', like those of 'The Flying Scotsman' and other trains, were assembled in a triple articulated set, with only four bogies under the three bodies, of first-class saloon, third-class saloon, and kitchen. This not only reduced the weight considerably, but with the jointing of the bodies over one bogie produced very smooth riding. 'The Silver Jubilee' had two 2-car twin coaches, and a triple articulated dining-car set. Our picture shows one of the 2-car sets, with the name of the train on the end corridor connection.

161 **Stanier streamlined Pacific;** London Midland and Scottish Railway. In the coronation year of King George VI, 1937, the L.M.S.R., like the L.N.E.R. built special trains for the Anglo-Scottish service, and while the L.N.E.R. named their train simply 'The Coronation', and decked it in two shades of blue, Cambridge and Garter, the L.M.S.R. in recognition of the names of their existing Scottish services – Royal Scot, Midday Scot, and Night Scot – named their train the Coronation Scot. When first introduced the engines and coaches of the Coronation Scot were painted in a dark blue like that of the Caledonian Railway locomotives in days before the more familiar bright blue was adopted. In 1939, however, when more locomotives of

the so-called 'Princess-Coronation' class were authorized, five were built in the original streamlined style and five non-streamlined. All were named after Duchesses, but the new streamlined engines were finished in standard L.M.S.R. 'red', with gold stripes, instead of the dark blue. One of the new engines, No. 6229 *Duchess of Hamilton* was selected to represent the L.M.S.R. at Chicago World Fair, which was to be held in the summer of 1939, and in view of the special nature of the visit to the U.S.A. the number and name of this new engine were exchanged with that of the original streamliner, No. 6220 *Coronation.* The latter engine, still in blue livery, ran for some considerable time as 6229 *Duchess of Hamilton.* Further engines of the 'Duchess' class were built from 1939 onwards and named after cities. These were streamlined, and our picture shows the first of the new batch, the *City of Birmingham.*

162 **'Coronation Scot' stock for New York World's Fair.**
The visit of the L.M.S.R. locomotive and train to the U.S.A. in 1939 was made the occasion of quite an extensive tour of the eastern railways, with the train travelling under its own steam, and coaches included in the formation were not representative of the 'Coronation Scot' service as normally operated between Euston and Glasgow, but representative of the different types of rolling stock worked on both day and night trains at that time. It included a sleeping car, and a special buffet lounge. Hauled by the red streamlined engine named *Coronation* specially for the tour, the train from landing at Baltimore visited Washington, Philadelphia, Pittsburgh, Cincinnati, St. Louis, Chicago, Detroit, Cleveland, Buffalo, Albany, Boston and, finally, to New York, for exhibition at the World's Fair. In the course of this tour the train travelled over nine different American railways. But the Fair lasted until October 1, and by that time Britain was at war with Germany. Engine and train were thus marooned in the U.S.A. Arrangements were made to get the engine back to this country, where it was urgently needed for the wartime traffic. But the coaches remained in America for the whole of the war. In the U.S.A. railwaymen and railway enthusiasts came to calling the marooned train 'The Refugee Scot'!

163 **Great Western Railway coat of arms.**
The Great Western Railway, as incorporated in 1835, was no more than a line connecting Bristol with London. I have purposely put the two cities in that order, because the origin of the project lay at the western end, and it was, appropriately, in Bristol that some of the major functions in connection with the centenary celebrations in 1935 took place. The Great Western 'coat of arms' thus consisted of nothing more than the arms of London and Bristol. There was perhaps an even greater significance in this very simple device, in that originally very little consideration was given to any intermediate business, and many towns that might have been served were by-passed in the interests of having a straight, direct route suitable for making fast time from end to end. Even when the Great Western came to incorporate such important concerns as the 'Bristol and Exeter', the 'South Devon', the 'Cornwall Railway' and others in Wales and the West Midlands, the insignia was not changed. When it was applied to engine and carriage decoration, the first form that was used for about twenty-five years had the arms of the two cities encircled within a garter, after the fashion of so many of the railways in pre-grouping days. But from the nineteen-thirties the garter was not used, and the two arms were displayed alone, on engine tenders and carriages alike.

164 **Coat of Arms;** London Midland and Scottish Railway.
The constituent companies of the L.M.S.R. had between them a wonderful collection of heraldic devices. Some, undoubtedly, had no heraldic justification it is true, but in looking through the coloured illustrations in this book and studying the coats of arms of the London and North Western Railway, the Midland, the Caledonian, the Highland, the Furness, the Lancashire and Yorkshire, to say nothing of the North London, and the North Staffordshire, it could be well imagined a little difficult to devise something that would contain heraldic significance of the great amalgamation that had taken place. One could not, for example, take the devices of the constituents and group them in one, as the South Eastern and the London Chatham and Dover did, within the encircling garter of the Managing Committee. Instead, the L.M.S.R. adopted a very simple device including only the arms of London, the rose of England, and the thistle of Scotland. When the locomotive livery had been decided upon, and the style of the former Midland Railway adopted, the coat of arms of the L.M.S.R. was put on the cabs of express passenger locomotives, as the Midland one had been done, but in later years when the engine numbers were put on the engines, rather than in huge transfer figures on the tenders, the coat of arms had to be dispensed with, and it was then used only on main-line carriages.

165 **Coat of Arms;** London and North Eastern Railway.
After grouping, the L.N.E.R. – an amalgamation of the Great Northern, Great Central, Great Eastern, North Eastern, North British and Great North of Scotland Railways, together with some smaller lines – adopted what was without a doubt the most beautiful and appropriate heraldic device ever associated with a British railway company. The full heraldic description is:

> 'Argent on a Cross Gules between the first and fourth quarters a Griffin seqreant Sable in the second a Rose of the second leaved and slipped proper and in third quarter a Thistle also leaved and slipped proper the Castle of Edinburgh proper between four Lions passant guardant Or And for the Crest On a Wreath of the Colours Issuant from Clouds of Steam the figure of Mercury proper'.

The motto 'Forward' was, of course, that of the Great Central Railway. When this coat of arms appeared as a colour plate in *The Railway Magazine* early in 1924 enthusiasts naturally expected that this beautiful device would soon be displayed on locomotive and carriages, as the previous insignia of the North Eastern, Great Central and other constituents had so lavishly been done in the past. Alas no! It was painted by hand on the *Flying Scotsman* engine when decked in all its glory for exhibition at Wembley in 1924 and 1925; but no transfer was ever made, and the only other use of the coat of arms was on a small inspection engine, specially painted for hauling the directors' saloon after World War II.

166 **Coat of Arms;** Pullman Car Company.
Ever since their first introduction on day services in the South of England, in 1876, Pullmans have been synonymous with an extra luxury in travel. Large bogie carriages, with high clerestory roofs, stood apart from the ordinary run of British passenger carriages, and it was their influence that could be seen in the luxurious carriage developments on the Great Northern Railway, and in the London and North London dining car around the turn of the century. But it was, above all, the inception, in November 1908, of the Brighton Company's

Southern Belle that set the final seal upon the popularity of the Pullman car for luxurious day travel, with buffet facilities. From that time onwards the Pullman cars running in this country, with the exception of those on the South Eastern and Chatham Railway, were painted in a dignified livery of chocolate and cream, using a rather darker brown than that of the two-tone Great Western carriages. The first-class cars were mostly given female Christian names, but the third class only numbers; but all were alike in bearing the handsome Pullman coat of arms. This was displayed also inside the cars. Its rich colouring, on the background of the dark brown coach bodies, stood out very well. With the passing of the steam age, and the introduction of different kinds of Pullman trains, a different version of the device has been adopted. It is considerably less attractive than the old one, though no doubt more suited to the new conditions.

167 **Thompson Class 'A2' Pacific;** London and North Eastern Railway.
During the war years difficulty was experienced in maintaining the conjugated valve gear of the Gresley three-cylinder 'Pacific'. And although the design was, in ordinary circumstances, one of the most successful ever to be produced in Great Britain, Sir Nigel's successor, Edward Thompson decided for his future designs to use three sets of valve gear, and so to dispose the cylinders in relation to the driving axles that all three connecting rods were of equal length. This led to a spacing of the wheels that looked a little odd. The arrangement was tried out during the war on some Pacifics that were rebuilt from the Gresley 'Cock o' the North' class 2-8-2s; but our picture shows one of the post-war 'A2' class built new at Doncaster, and mostly named, like previous L.N.E.R. 'Pacifics' after racehorses. The new 'A2' engines proved fast and powerful machines, and although their coupled wheels were only 6 ft. 2 in. diameter against the 6 ft. 8 in. of the Gresley 'Pacifics' they were very successfully used on the main line between King's Cross and Newcastle. Nevertheless, when A. H. Peppercorn in turn succeeded Edward Thompson as Chief Mechanical Engineer of the L.N.E.R., he did not perpetuate the 'odd' wheel spacing, but reverted to the Gresley spacing while retaining the three sets of valve gear, instead of the Gresley conjugated motion. Even so, neither the Thompson nor the Peppercorn 'Pacifics' came to supersede the Gresleys on the fastest and the most important duties.

168 **Bulleid's 'Austerity' 0-6-0 goods engine;** Southern Railway.
During World War II additional goods engines were required on the Southern Railway, but of a weight that would permit of their being used over almost the entire system. A good general purpose 0-6-0 existed in the Maunsell 'Q' class, which met requirements so far as weight was concerned. But Bulleid considered that greater boiler capacity would be an advantage for the wartime traffic, so he reconsidered the design using the largest boiler that could be produced for such a chassis from existing tools. The flanging blocks for the 'Lord Nelson' 4-6-0 were found suitable, and a design worked out for a much larger boiler than that used on the Maunsell 'Q' class 0-6-0. If the engine had been finished in conventional style the weight would have exceeded the limits imposed, and so every item that was not absolutely necessary was discarded. As will be seen in our picture there were no running plates, no wheel-splashers, and the outer plates containing the boiler lagging were finished in a most unorthodox manner. 'Austerity' was certainly the word for these queer-looking engines, which looked as though they were not finished. All the essentials were there however, and they proved excellent

if somewhat inelegant tools for the wartime traffic.

169 **'Schools' class 4-4-0 in wartime livery;** Southern Railway.
The conditions of wartime imposed many difficult circumstances upon the locomotive departments of the British railways. Some of the workshops were engaged in direct production of munitions, others had their labour forces greatly reduced, and all the time difficulty was experienced in obtaining the choice materials specified in pre-war days for some of the important working parts of locomotives. Even so it was vitally necessary to keep the locomotive stocks in good working order. The tasks of express passenger engines like the 'Schools' were not so onerous in themselves as those demanded of them in pre-war days; but the wheels had to be kept turning with reliability, and when the time came for overhaul no effort could be spared to impart to repaired engines the spanking finish of peacetime. They were given the minimum necessary to preserve the metal, and that minimum meant nothing more than a coat of plain black without any lining. Little, if any, time could be spared at the sheds for real cleaning, and plain black was the most logical and serviceable 'colour'. Nevertheless, shorn of their pre-war finery, the handsome proportions of the 'Schools' class engine were still amply evident. Our picture, showing engine No. 930 *Radley*, is of one of those fitted by Mr. Bulleid with the five-nozzled multiple jet blastpipe, and having an unusually large chimney in consequence.

170 **London Midland Class '5' 4-6-0 with Caprotti valve gear;** British Railways.
After the end of World War II, in the few years that elapsed before the nationalization of the railways the L.M.S.R. made a number of experiments with accessories aiming at improved availability, more efficient performance, and a lessening of maintenance work. Taking the Stanier Class '5' 4-6-0 as a basis, a number of engines were built with experimental variations, so arranged that comparison could readily be made one with another. There was, for example, a straight trial of driving axles with plain against roller bearings, and other engines were fitted with different forms of valve gear as alternatives to the long-established Walschaerts radial gear. The engine shown in our picture was one of a batch fitted with the British-Caprotti form of poppet valve gear, and also fitted with roller bearings, while a single engine of the Class '5' group was equipped with Stephenson's link motion, outside. In these comparative tests, also, some engines were equipped with twin blastpipes and double chimneys. It cannot be said that anything positive came out of the valve gear trials, because Walschaerts was generally adopted as standard for the new British Railways locomotives. But for high-powered and medium-powered machines the advantage of roller bearings was clearly established. Our picture shows one of the ex-L.M.S.R. 4-6-0s in the first British Railways style of painting with the original number surmounted by the letter M to indicate London Midland Region.

171–2 **Upper Quadrant Signals.**
The lower quadrant signal had become one of the great institutions of the British steam railways. It was so simple and reliable, and so well understood by railwaymen and the travelling public alike! Those who travelled abroad could well be mystified by the curious array of signs and signals displayed on some foreign railways: semaphores that moved in odd and unexpected directions; boards and diamond signs in different colours that would suddenly startle the onlooker by moving round with a great clatter. The lower

quadrant semaphore was such an institution in Great Britain that the mere suggestion of changing it was enough to arouse the most acute controversy. Yet in the years just before the outbreak of World War I there were pioneer spirits who felt that our code of signalling was growing inadequate. There had been one or two bad collisions through drivers disregarding signals, and with the development of three-position signalling in the United States some serious consideration was given to make similar changes here. It was essential that a three-position semaphore should work through the upper quadrant: horizontal for 'stop', inclined upwards for 'caution', and vertically upwards for 'clear'. An electrically-worked signal of this type was installed at Paddington, and towards the end of the war a contract was let for a complete installation of them at Victoria on the S.E.&C.R. side of the station. After the war the development of the colour light signal made this a much simpler way of providing three indications from one signal, with the now-familiar red, amber and green lights, that three-position semaphore signals made no further headway in Great Britain, though British contractors installed them in considerable numbers overseas. But an important sequel to the three-position controversy was the decision, by three out of the four big companies operated by the grouping of 1923, to standardize in future upon the upper quadrant type of semaphore for all ordinary mechanical working. This was done because in the first place the mechanism could be made much lighter. The arm returned to the danger position by gravity, and it was no longer necessary to build into the spectacle a heavy counterweight to ensure that the arm returned to the horizontal position if there was any mishap to the mechanism, or if the operating wire broke. Upper quadrant semaphores could readily be applied to existing posts, and our pictures show groups of signals on both wood and lattice posts. The latter (reference 172), was a location on the former Great Northern Railway, where the upper quadrant arms had replaced the 'somersault' type. Of the grouped railways only the Great Western stood apart, and continued to use lower quadrant semaphores, many of which are still in service today.

173–4 **Groups of semaphore signals;** South Eastern and Chatham Railway.

The traditional lower quadrant signal was a picturesque thing in itself – always kept smartly painted, and having for the keen observer many features of individual interest as between the practice of the various railway companies. But on many railways the picturesque aspect of semaphore signals as such was greatly enhanced by the way they were multiplied and grouped in the approaches to large stations and junctions. There was at least one semaphore for each route a train could take, and if one added shunting and 'calling-on' arms, and the frequent mounting of distant arms on the same post as the stop signals associated with the same route one could have a truly extraordinary array. Two very large assemblies are illustrated under references 191 and 192, but the present pictures relate more particularly to the structures on which some of these arrays were mounted. It goes without saying that the more signals to be displayed the more complicated would be the track layout. Space on the ground would be at a premium, and in many cases quite large gantries and cantilevers had to be built in order to permit of the semaphore being mounted reasonably near to the tracks to which they applied. Of course this could not always be done to the ideal extent; but the configurations had to be designed so that the indications displayed could not be mistaken by the driver of a train.

Nevertheless, the driver had to 'learn the road', and sign a book expressing his familiarity with it; and that in many cases meant memorizing the signal configurations at large centres. The assembly (reference 173) is a most interesting one, and relates to the starting point from a main-line platform in a terminal station from which a train could proceed to any one of four routes. The semaphores by their positioning indicate the geographical direction – that is the arm farthest to the left signifies the route farthest to the left, and so on. The design of the supporting posts is interesting. It was necessary to have the arms as near as possible above the roofs of the carriages, and so the mechanism for working them was placed above. The second illustration (reference 174) includes a group with a different significance. All the arms in reference 173 related to one departure line and all routes were of equal importance. In No. 174, the subsidiary posts rising from the main cross-girder indicate that two separate running lines are involved, one on each side of the central post, and the arrangement of the semaphore above indicates a bifurcation, in each case with the left-hand route of greater importance than the right-hand one. Associated with each of these running lines is a shunt signal, with a ringed arm. The pictures 173 and 174 show two different styles of arm painting: that in 173 was the later one adopted on the Southern Railway generally after grouping, while the semaphores of the constituent companies remained in service. That in 174 was the standard South Eastern and Chatham style, with a white disc, instead of the more usual white band on the red blade.

175 **Fowler 2-6-4 fast passenger tank engine;** London Midland and Scottish Railway.
In 1927 the former Midland Railway drawing office was engaged on the design of a new express tank engine that would be used at all large centres where fast and heavy residential passenger services were operated: around London, Manchester, Birmingham and Glasgow in particular. The design was conceived on traditional Midland lines, but at the last minute, fortunately, some changes were made in the design of the valve gear which resulted in an extraordinarily efficient and free-running engine. On the Euston–Watford services speeds of 80 m.p.h. were common on the trains running non-stop over this 17½ miles. Although having coupled wheels no larger than 5 ft. 9 in. which gave them the capacity for quick acceleration, they ran with the freedom of an express-passenger engine, with wheels one foot larger in diameter. As originally built the first examples were painted in Midland red, as shown in our picture; but later ones were painted black. A total of 95 was built to the original design, followed in 1933 by a further 30 which differed in having side-window cabs. They fulfilled every expectation, doing splendid work on the local trains from Euston and St. Pancras, and on the fast trains between the Glasgow termini of Central and St. Enoch and the Clyde coast resorts. After Sir William Stanier had succeeded to the post of Chief Mechanical Engineer of the L.M.S.R. many more 2-6-4 tank engines were built, though these later ones had the Stanier type of taper boiler. Eventually there were 645 engines of this wheel arrangement on the L.M.S.R.

176 **Thompson 2-6-4 mixed-traffic tank engine, Class 'L1';** London and North Eastern Railway.
In his programme for the standardization of the steam locomotive stock of the L.N.E.R., Edward Thompson made a particular feature of the use of existing standard parts and manufacturing equipment. A powerful suburban tank engine was needed, to take over duties on which relatively old engines had previously

been employed, and this new design was derived from the 5 ft. 2 in. 2-6-0 class 'K1', which in turn originally was produced by rebuilding one of Sir Nigel Gresley's three cylinder 2-6-0s of Class 'K4' with two cylinders and outside Walschaerts valve gear, in place of the previous conjugated gear. The same boiler, firebox, and frame design was used, and the new cylinders were also an existing standard. The 2-6-4 tank of 1945 was thus a tank-engine version of the 'K1', and a very solid and robust job it was, having a tractive effort of 32,080 lb against the 23,125 lb of the L.M.S.R. engine (reference 175). The difference between the two was that the L.N.E.R. was essentially a mixed-traffic engine, suitable for goods as well as passenger, and for use on services where heavy haulage capacity, rather than fast running was needed. Our picture shows one of these engines in the early style of painting used on British Railways, in lined black but before the totem had been introduced. More than 100 of these locomotives were built.

177 **Heavy mineral 2-8-2 tank engine;** '72XX' class, Great Western Railway.

In the year 1910 a useful addition was made to the standard locomotive types in use on the Great Western Railway. Churchward's original plan of complete standardization in 1901 included two tank-engine types, the 4-4-2 and the 2-6-2; but later the need was felt for a heavy mineral engine in South Wales that could handle loads equal to those worked by the main-line 2-8-0s, but were suited to short distance hauls. Thus the '42XX' 2-8-0 tank was put on the road. At a later period, between the two world wars, the increasing length of run on some of the coal train workings showed the need for a tank engine with greater coal capacity than the '42XX' class 2-8-0, and so a number of these powerful engines were rebuilt with larger coal bunkers, and altered to the 2-8-2 wheel arrangement. Our picture shows one of these handsome engines. Among other duties they work the coal trains from Severn Tunnel Junction to the Southern line, travelling via the outskirts of Bristol, Bath, Westbury and Warminster, to hand over to the Southern at Salisbury. Their coupled wheels are smaller even than those of the L.N.E.R. 'L1' class, only 4 ft. 7½ in., and in consequence they have the still higher tractive effort of 33,170 lb. This is the same as that of Churchward's 2-8-0 tanks of 1910, as the engine and boiler are identical. The only difference between the '42XX' and the '72XX' classes lies in the size of the coal bunker and in the wheel arrangement.

178 **'BR4' Standard 2-6-4 tank engine;** British Railways.

The six-coupled passenger tank engines on three out of the four British main-line railways of pre-nationalization days, the Great Western, the L.M.S.R. and the L.N.E.R., had proved so useful in fast short-distance service that a design of this general type seemed almost a certainty in the new range of standard classes that were in course of preparation for British Railways soon after nationalization. There were 2-6-2s on the Great Western and the L.N.E.R., and 2-6-4s on both the L.N.E.R. and L.M.S.R. Of these the Stanier type on the L.M.S.R. was best suited to general use in all parts of the country where steam-operated short distance services were operated; but while the familiar Stanier taper boiler and trapezoidal-shaped firebox was adopted with very little alteration the cylinders were made with a smaller diameter and longer stroke; 18 in. by 28 in., against 19 in. by 26 in. on the L.M.S.R. engines. The coupled wheels were slightly smaller, and this produced an engine with slightly higher tractive effort. The new engines, which were first introduced in 1951, were numbered from 80000 upwards, and they were styled in accordance with uniform 'look' persisting through all the new medium-powered classes in the British Railways standard range. They proved excellent engines in service, rapid in acceleration, very fast, and light on coal. They were certainly an admirable climax to the chain of development of the express-tank service for residential and medium-distance service.

179 **Furness Railway coat of arms.**
This was one of the most beautiful of all railway coats of arms, and unlike some devices – which though picturesque had a rather doubtful heraldic justification – it was most appropriate to the district served, and to some of the personal associations involved. The Furness Railway had nevertheless, a twofold function: to serve the rapidly expanding industries of Barrow and to provide transport for the iron ore in which the Furness and West Cumberland districts were at one time very rich; and secondly, to develop tourist traffic to the English Lake District. The intense industrialism of Barrow, and of many smaller towns along the coast of the Irish Sea finds no place on the Furness Railway coat of arms; instead it is the historic associations of the district that are depicted. The Madonna and Child, which forms the centre-piece, is part of the arms of the Abbot of Furness. The ruins of the once-great Cistercian abbey of Furness lie close to the railway by Furness Abbey station, in the oddly named Vale of Deadly Nightshade! The motto *Cavendo Tutus* – advance with caution – is that of the Cavendish family whose head, the Duke of Devonshire, always took a very active interest in Furness Railway affairs. The coat of arms, in its delicate detail, looked equally fine on the panels of the royal blue carriages, and on the locomotives in their distinctive 'iron ore' red livery.

180 **Somerset and Dorset Joint Railway coat of arms.**
The garter of this attractive device encircles the arms of the City of Bath, on the left, and of the ancient borough of Dorchester. But although these two places are truly representative of the counties of Somerset and Dorset the railway itself never extended to anywhere near Dorchester, and it was many years after its first incorporation that the line reached Bath. The railway was originally an amalgamation of two still-smaller concerns: the Somerset Central, and the Dorset Central, and this amalgamated company had a line that extended from Highbridge on the Bristol Channel to Wimborne. It crossed the London and South Western main line at Templecombe, and eventually linked-up with the same company at Poole, and gained access to Bournemouth West. The amalgamation took place in 1862, and it was the result of a proposal to extend northwards from Evercreech to Bath that interested the Midland Railway, because it opened up the possibility of through services between the Midlands and Bournemouth. The line to Bath was completed in 1874, but so depleted were the funds of the company as a result of the heavy cost of building this line through difficult country, that for some time it hovered on the brink of bankruptcy. Eventually an agreement was concluded in which the Midland and the London and South Western took a joint lease of the line, in 1876. The joint ownership continued, indeed, through the grouping period, between the London Midland and Scottish, and the Southern. After nationalization it continued for eighteen years as part of British Railways, but it was finally closed in March 1966.

181 **Hull and Barnsley Railway coat of arms.**
This very enterprising local railway was born out of a desire to break the monopoly of the rich and powerful North Eastern Railway, which had the country between the Humber and the Tweed to itself. In Victorian times there was a very large export trade in coal from England to the Baltic and Scandinavian countries, and the coal-owners of Yorkshire, shipping through Hull, were very dissatisfied with the treatment they were receiving from the North Eastern. The coat of arms of the Hull and Barnsley Railway is a piece of history in itself, for it not only includes the arms of Hull and Barnsley, but it combined also the winged wheel of the railway with the dolphins of the Hull docks. The date, 1880, was the year in which the Act of Parliament authorizing the line received the Royal assent. Actually the railway was not opened until five years later. In Hull the line had three terminal stations – two at the docksides, and a central passenger station in Cannon Street. At the western end it did not reach Barnsley on its own metals; the last two miles were run over the tracks of the Midland. But it made connection with many of the South Yorkshire collieries, and it was from these that its principal traffic came. A fast passenger service was run between Sheffield and Hull, and the distinctive black engines of the Hull and Barnsley Railway were to be seen in the Midland station at Sheffield. In the coat of arms, the shield of Hull with its three crowns is a reminder of the full title of that city – Kingston-upon-Hull.

182 **North Staffordshire Railway coat of arms.**
The North Staffordshire Railway was the outcome of one of the earliest railway projects in Great Britain. Birmingham was the focal point of much earlier railway promoting in the Midlands, and at the time that the London and Birmingham Railway was being discussed and the great trunk line to connect Birmingham with the Liverpool and Manchester Railway was also under active discussion, plans were also being prepared for a line between Manchester and Birmingham. Railway politics north of Birmingham became complicated and difficult in earlier days and eventually the Manchester and Birmingham project, instead of being an independent concern, running through the Potteries and serving the growing industrial districts that, even then, were beginning to cluster round Stoke-on-Trent, became watered down into nothing more than a relatively short-cut of a line from Manchester to join the Grand Junction main line at Crewe. Nevertheless, the original project of a line through the Potteries was still actively canvassed and it formed the nucleus of the North Staffordshire Railway system, which eventually formed part of a most important alternative through-route from Manchester to London via Stoke-on-Trent. The promoters were anxious to have a fast direct route, and consequently a number of towns in the Potteries were by-passed and had later to be served by branch lines which, of course, became something of an embarrassment with increasing traffic and the need to provide numerous feeder services to the main line. Although the North Staffordshire Railway maintained its independence to the very end of pre-grouping days, and it played a very considerable part in providing through-train workings to destinations far beyond its own territory, its activities were above all centred upon Stoke; and it is the arms of the City of Stoke-on-Trent, together with the traditional 'knot' of Staffordshire that forms the pervading *motif* of the handsome coat of arms adopted by this railway. It was carried on all the passenger and local tank engines and in earlier days some of them carried the 'Staffordshire Knot' as well.

183 *The Princess Elizabeth* **engine in black;** London Midland Region, British Railways.
Immediately after nationalization, in 1948, British Railways had to give consideration to the liveries to be adopted as a future standard, and a number of experimental styles were tried. In the pictures (references 183–6) are shown four styles three of which did not survive very long. There was a demonstration, at which express-passenger engines in various colours were slowly steamed past members of the Railway Executive; but one of those that created the biggest impression was the *Princess Elizabeth,* one of Sir William Stanier's famous 'Princess Royal' class 'Pacifics', which had been painted in the colours of the former London and North Western Railway; a magnificent glossy black, lined-out in red, cream and grey, to the tradition of the Crewe Works of twenty-five years earlier. Of course there is no doubt that a black locomotive, like a well-groomed black motor-car, can look superb, and on that day the *Princess Elizabeth* created a deep impression. But it was felt that to paint all British Railways locomotives in black would be to create a bad public image, and so the use of 'blackberry black', as it used to be called in L.N.W.R. days was confined to second-line express passenger, and mixed-traffic engines, and blue was selected, as a first choice, for the largest express-passenger classes.

184 **'Merchant Navy' class 4-6-2 in standard blue;** Southern Region, British Railways.
The shade of blue finally adopted for the large express-passenger engines was not finally determined after that first demonstration at Addison Road, and a number of engines were decked in the dark blue shown in the reference No. 185. The light blue, which was standardized in 1949 and used for a few years afterwards, was closely similar in its tone to the blue of the Caledonian Railway, but with black underframes and black wheels it did not have the same beautiful effect as the Scottish colour scheme of old, in which the wheels were blue, and the valances, and tender frames purple lake. Even so, the British Railways engines mostly looked very well in the blue. In addition to the 'Merchant Navy' class illustrated, the blue was applied to all the Stanier Pacifics of the former L.M.S.R., to all the Gresley 'Pacifics', to the new Peppercorn Pacifics of the Eastern and North Eastern Region, and to the ex-G.W.R. 'King' class 4-6-0s. It must be admitted however that blue did not suit these latter engines. Their lavish array of brass and copper work was admirably set-off by the traditional Brunswick green of the Great Western Railway; but it did not go at all well with the blue, and I think everyone concerned with those engines was glad when the blue was abandoned by British Railways.

185 **A Gresley 'A3' Pacific in experimental dark blue;** Eastern and North Eastern Region.
The dark blue style of painting was no more than an experimental phase, when an attempt was made to secure the reaction of the public to some of the proposed liveries. It was endeavoured to keep the repainted engines available to work trains of coaching stock in the new colours, when complete rakes of repainted coaches, some in chocolate and cream, and some in the oft-derided 'plum and spilt-milk', were run on certain named express passenger trains. The dark-blue engines, like the L.M.S.R. *Coronation* of 1937, were reminiscent of the Caledonian in the late-Victorian era, though lacking the distinction of the purple underframes. But the British Railways experimental dark blue also included the old L.N.W.R. style of lining-out with red edging to the boiler bands, and red, cream and grey lining around the tenders and the cab

sides. The repainting was done before the British Railways totem device had been designed, and the majority of the engines to be treated had the name BRITISH RAILWAYS painted in full on the tenders. In my opinion the dark blue would have looked better with a plain black and white lining-out. It was not applied to all engines of the Class '8' power classification; but 'Kings', 'Merchant Navy' 4-6-2s, 'Duchesses and Gresley Pacifics of both 'A3' and 'A4' classes were so bedecked for a few months.

186 **A 'Castle' class 4-6-0 in the 'experimental' light green;** Western Region, British Railways.
While trials were being made of dark blue as a livery for the largest express-passenger engines, during 1948 and 1949 certain selected express-passenger engines of lesser tractive capacity were painted in a livery of pale green. Included in this group were some ex-G.W.R. 'Castle' class 4-6-0s; ex-Southern 'Lord Nelson' and some ex-L.M.S.R. rebuilt 'Royal Scots'. Whether by accident or design the basic colour, which was a beautiful shade of green, was closely similar to that used at one time on the Adams express engines of the London and South Western Railway, and it was perhaps no more than a coincidence that of the three types chosen to display this experimental style the 'Lord Nelson's looked incomparably the best. But incorporated with this pale green was once again the old Crewe type of lining-out, in red, grey and cream. One presumes the idea was to have the same style of lining-out, whether the basic colour of the engine was black, blue or green. But what looked superb on a black engine, was less effective on a dark-blue one, and perfectly horrible on light green! Fortunately this particular experiment did not last long. At a distance the light-green engines, particularly the 'Lord Nelsons', looked pleasant at the head of a train of coaches in the experimental 'plum and spilt milk'; but closer acquaintance did not confirm that good impression, so far as the engine was concerned.

187 **Double-chimneyed 'King' class 4-6-0;** Western Region, British Railways.
In the last years of steam various measures were taken to improve the performance of existing locomotives, some definitely advanced in years, to enable them to carry on until steam would be superseded by one of the newer forms of motive power. The 'King' class 4-6-0s were introduced on the Great Western Railway in 1927, and for more than twenty years they had remained completely unchanged in their design. After World War II some modifications were made to the draughting to enable them to use more effectively the poorer grades of coal that were then coming into increasing use for British Railways; and then after a life of nearly thirty years, spent entirely in the heaviest express passenger service, the whole class of 30 engines was subjected to an important, yet simply made, modification by the fitting of twin blastpipes and double chimneys. This certainly made a definite improvement to the performance of the engines and, in conjunction with some structural renewal of the frames at the front end, gave the class a useful additional lease of life, enabling them to continue in heavy passenger traffic to the end of the steam era. Our picture shows one of these modified engines in the standard dark-green livery adopted for all major express-passenger classes in the last years of steam. It was almost exactly the same as the old Great Western standard, except for certain minor differences in lining.

188 **Standard main-line coaching stock;** British Railways.
After the various experimental liveries for locomotives and carriages tried out soon after nationalization, including the pre-

viously mentioned chocolate and cream, and the 'plum and spilt milk' the decision was taken to adopt a two-tone colour scheme that was entirely new, having cream upper panels, and bodies in a bright cherry red. This was certainly a very distinguished style, but one cannot say more than that about it. Coaches so repainted stood out vividly whether in the drab surroundings of an industrial area or out in the fairest countryside. But it was a synthetic colour scheme. It did not blend with the natural surroundings like the chocolate and cream of the Great Western, like the various varnished teak styles of pre-grouping days, or like the beautiful crimson lake of the Midland, which always seemed so particularly appropriate to the moorland landscapes of Derbyshire and the Northern Pennines. The earliest British Railways standard coaches were built at a time when austerity still had the railway economy in its grasp, and in comparison with some coaches of pre-war days the new stock was spartan in its appointments, and simple in its engineering detail. They were 'economy class' vehicles rather than a synthesis of all that was best in previous practice; but they served their day, and have now been largely displaced from the more important trains by later designs.

189 **Rebuilt 'Royal Scot' class 4-6-0 in standard green livery;** British Railways.

In discussing the experimental colours tried after nationalization, under references 183 to 186, I referred to the distinction originally made between the largest express passenger engines, and a selected group of lesser types. The former were originally painted blue, while after trial liveries the lesser group was finished in a dark Brunswick green, with lining closely similar to that of the former Great Western Railway. Eventually the blue was abandoned, and Brunswick green adopted for all express classes. The 'Royal Scot' class engine shown in our picture is typical of the engines, having the number in transfer figures on the cab sides. The dark green was applied to all 'Pacifics'; to the 'Sandringhams' class 4-6-0s; to the 'Lord Nelsons' and 'King Arthurs' – though not, to the disappointment of many enthusiasts, to the 'Schools'. On the London Midland Region, in addition to the 'Royal Scots' it was applied to the Stanier 'Jubilee' class three-cylinder 4-6-0s, and to the 'Patriots', while on the Western Region it was used on 'Castles', 'Stars', 'Counties' and 'Halls'. In still later years some of the ex-L.M.S.R. 'Pacifics' were painted in red once again – the wheel having come full circle, through red, wartime black, two shades of blue, B.R. green, and finally back to red. But the greatest diversity of painting that was applied to any British locomotives was that on the Gresley 'A4' streamlined 'Pacifics'. In pre-war years the first four were silver, and later changed to Garter blue. A further batch was originally finished in standard L.N.E.R. apple-green like the non-streamlined 'Pacifics' and other express passenger engines. These were all changed to Garter blue in the last pre-war years. Then came the wartime unlined black when economy was carried to the extent of contracting the initials on the tender from L.N.E.R. to N.E.! Immediately after the war Garter blue was restored, to be followed by the experimental B.R. blues. Finally, these engines ended their careers in the dark Brunswick green: seven different styles in all, though not every individual engine had all seven!

190 **Standard main-line coaching stock with Commonwealth bogies.**

One of the problems faced by the engineers of British Railways was to provide good modern rolling stock that would give long service and a satisfactory ride with the minimum of attention. In the early days of nationalization, when express-train schedules were being speeded-up, adverse comment was frequently made upon the poor riding of the stock, and it was compared unfavourably to this or that design of pre-war coach, all of which were usually smooth at the highest speeds. What was not generally realized was that those earlier coaches had much closer and continuous maintenance, whereas in post-war years neither the finance nor the staff were forthcoming to provide such attention. A great deal of research in coach suspension and bogie design was undertaken in post-nationalization days to produce vehicles that would maintain their initial standards of riding over long periods with the minimum of attention, and one outcome was the fitting – largely as an interim measure – of many new coaches with the 'Commonwealth' design of bogie, while new designs were being worked out for future standards. The coach illustrated is typical of the second phase of British standard coach design, when 'Midland red' had once again been adopted as the standard livery for all except the Southern Region. This coach is representative of the very last days of steam, and it is a sign of the changing times that it is a 'dual heated', with provision either for steam or electric heating, while the prefix to the number on the body side 'SC', indicates that it is attached to Scottish Region. The distinctive yellow covers to the axle-boxes indicate the use of roller bearings. Since the introduction of these vehicles yet another change has been made in British standard coach livery to a pale grey and blue: but this takes us beyond the era of steam railways.

191 **Large signal gantry, with somersault arms;** Great Northern Railway.
In describing the interesting configurations of semaphore signals used on the South Eastern and Chatham Railway (references 173 and 174), mention was made of still larger assemblies, and the present picture shows a typical gantry on the Great Northern Railway. It was one located at Red Bank, Doncaster, and shows an interesting grouping of the arms appropriate to the tracks below. The southbound main line, used by all passenger trains ran beneath the overhanging cantilever portion at the right-hand end. The tall 'doll' post at the extreme end related to the main line, with a 'distant' arm below the stop arm for the direct line to London. The two 'distant' arms immediately to the left indicated divergencies at the next signal box ahead to other routes. The other four tracks, two under each span of the gantry, were entirely goods lines, and the signals were used to regulate the movements of departing goods trains for the south. Beyond the gantry the goods trains left the extensive marshalling yards that lie on the south side of Doncaster station, and entered upon the main lines either towards London, towards the Eastern Counties, or westwards to the Yorkshire coalfields. In Great Northern days the distant as well as the stop signals had the blades painted red and the distant arms did not have the distinction of the chevron, instead of a plain white band. In later L.N.E.R. days the 'distant' arms on this gantry were painted yellow, with a black chevron, though retaining their somersault action. The main-line signals on the extreme right show the more usual angle to which these arms cleared.

192 **The great signal gantry at Rugby;** London and North Western Railway.
It would perhaps be an overstatement to suggest that this was the most famous signal gantry that ever existed; but certainly it was one of the best known, because of its great height and for the number of semaphore arms it carried, a

grand total of 44. There are actually two gantries, with the lower group of signals precisely duplicating the upper set. The reasons for this duplication will be explained later. Taking the grouping of the doll posts, these it will be seen, fall into three groups, corresponding to the three running lines approaching Rugby from the south – main line, Northampton line, and Peterborough line. Trains approaching on the main line could be routed to any one of three ways: into the goods lines, over the through-main line, or into the down-main platform, indicated by the three doll posts on the left-hand end of the gantry. Trains from the Northampton and Peterborough lines, as well as being routed to any one of the three just-mentioned lines could also be terminated in either of the two-bay platforms, so that additional semaphores are provided for these, to the right of the three through-running signals. Originally there was only the lower gantry, with 22 arms; but when the Great Central Railway constructed its London Extension line in 1899 its route crossed the tracks of the London and North Western Railway just to the south of Rugby station, and its massive girder bridge was built immediately behind the great 22 arms gantry. The existence of the elaborate criss-cross lattice work immediately behind the semaphore would have made sighting of them difficult, and so a duplicate gantry was built on which the semaphores mounted at a much higher level could be sighted against a sky background, well above the Great Central viaduct. As a condition for granting permission for the G.C.R. to cross their line at Rugby the North Western required the Great Central not only to bear the expense of duplicating all the semaphores, but to pay for the cost of maintaining them.

193 **Class 'BR6' Pacific 'Clan' class;** British Railways.

In the range of standard locomotives introduced by the nationalized British Railways a need was felt for a locomotive of less power, and lighter axle loading than the well-known 'Britannia' class, that would undertake duties previously worked by such engines as the ex-L.M.S.R. 'Jubilee' and 'Patriot' class 4-6-0s, but which would be better suited to burning an inferior grade of coal. The new engines were therefore built of the 'Pacific' type, with large, wide fireboxes, and all the modern appliances for lessening shed duties and maintenance work, in the form of self-cleaning smokeboxes, rocking firegrates, hopper ashpans, and roller bearings on all axles. As the duties for which these engines were originally to be drafted were based upon Glasgow, in working the through-expresses between that city and Manchester and Liverpool they were given the names of Highland 'Clans', thus perpetuating some of the most famous names from the railways of pre-grouping days in Scotland. The 'BR6' engines worked regularly through between Glasgow and Manchester, and did much good work. They were also extensively used on express duties in Scotland itself between Carlisle, Glasgow and Perth.

194 **'BR9' 2-10-0 with Franco-Crosti boiler;** British Railways.

The very last steam locomotive to be built was of the 'BR9' class 2-10-0, the *Evening Star*, and the class as a whole proved one of the most successful ever to run in this country, because of its extreme versatility. It was a simple, straightforward design, embodying those features which by long usage had been found to give that reliability in service that is so essential in railway working. Nevertheless, at a late stage in the history of the steam locomotive a trial was made on ten of these 'BR9' 2-10-0s of the Crosti type of boiler, which had been used with success on a considerable number of Italian locomotives. This aimed at securing increased thermal efficiency by pre-heating the water passing into the boiler. The exhaust steam from the cylinders instead of passing direct to the blastpipe as in a normal locomotive passed through long pipes to a blast chamber and thence to an exhaust outlet on the side of the boiler. These 'BR9' locomotives that were so fitted had a more orthodox look than their Italian counterparts, which had no chimney at all. In the British 2-10-0s the chimney on the front smokebox was used only when lighting-up. The exhaust normally from the pipe was on the side of the boiler. On British Railways experience with these ten locomotives was not sufficient to justify proceeding further with the experiment. Shortly after their construction the decision was taken to abandon steam altogether.

INDEX

Figures in heavy type are colour plates.
Figures in Roman, are descriptive notes.

		Ref. No.	*Page (colour)*	*Page (description)*
Auto-trains	Furness	**151**	**86**	171
	Great Northern	**152**	**86**	172
	Great Western	**154**	**87**	172
	Lancs. & Yorks	**153**	**87**	172
Carriages (Miscellaneous)	British Rlys. – standard	**188**	**104**	186
	standard with Commonwealth bogie	**190**	**105**	187
	Caledonian: 'Grampian'	**102**	**63**	152
	Observation Car *Maid of Morven*	**155**	**88**	173
	Cambrian:			
	Tri-compo. lavatory	**98**	**61**	151
	Cauldron wagon	**2**	**13**	109
	Furness: Inspection Saloon	**10**	**17**	112
	bogie saloon No. 1	**131**	**77**	164
	Great Central:			
	Vestibule car	**60**	**42**	134
	Compo. slip brake	**112**	**68**	157
	Open 'third'	**132**	**77**	164
	Great Eastern:			
	4 wh. 2nd suburban	**16**	**20**	115
	Corridor 'third'	**133**	**78**	165
	Great Northern:			
	4 wh. brake third	**8**	**16**	112
	Clerestory brake compo.	**62**	**43**	135
	Great Western:			
	ex-Monmouth tri-compo. 4 wh.	**6**	**15**	111
	local train 4 wh.	**17**	**21**	116
	Broad-gauge compo.	**21**	**23**	117
	Narrow-gauge clerestory	**78**	**51**	142
	Ocean saloon	**129**	**76**	163
	Pre-1914 70ft. third	**138**	**80**	167
	Bow-ended (Hawksworth)	**140**	**81**	168
	Centenary Riviera	**158**	**89**	174
	Highland:			
	Chariot-ended first	**44**	**34**	127
	Bogie corridor compo.	**80**	**52**	143
	Lancashire & Yorkshire:			
	Open brake third	**136**	**79**	166
	Liverpool & Manchester:			
	Traveller	**3**	**14**	109
	Third (no roof)	**4**	**14**	110
	London Brighton and South Coast:			
	Non.-corr. bogie third	**113**	**69**	157

Carriages (Miscellaneous) (*cont.*)	London Chatham and Dover:			
	Family Saloon	**46**	**35**	128
	London Midland and Scottish:			
	Open saloon	**148**	**84**	170
	Coronation Scot (U.S.A.)	**162**	**91**	176
	London & North Eastern:			
	Silver Jubilee train	**160**	**90**	175
	Coronation Observation car	**157**	**89**	174
	London & North Western:			
	Webb 'radial' 8 wh.	**19**	**22**	116
	Picnic saloon	**43**	**34**	127
	57ft. corr. compo.	**100**	**62**	152
	London & South Western:			
	Bogie 8 wh.	**50**	**37**	130
	Midland:			
	London suburban 4 wh.	**15**	**20**	115
	12 wh. brake third	**20**	**22**	117
	Bain, brake first	**116**	**70**	158
	Royal Saloon	**130**	**76**	164
	North British:			
	non-corr. 'first'	**82**	**53**	144
	North Eastern:			
	Corridor compo.	**118**	**71**	159
	North London:			
	4 wh. suburban	**18**	**21**	120
	North Union:			
	4 wh. first	**5**	**15**	110
	Somerset & Dorset:			
	4-wheeled	**45**	**35**	128
	Bogie-compo	**135**	**79**	166
	Southern:			
	standard corridor	**150**	**85**	171
	South Eastern:			
	Boat train 6 wh.	**22**	**23**	118
	South Eastern & Chatham:			
	Continental boat train 8 wh.	**48**	**36**	129
	Tri-compo. corr. brake	**97**	**61**	150
	West Coast Joint Stock:			
	brake first (corridor)	**76**	**50**	141
	early 8 wh.	**28**	**26**	120
Club Carriages	L.N.W.R. Manchester-Llandudno	**36**	**30**	124
	M.R. Bradford-Morecambe	**37**	**31**	124
Coats of Arms	Caledonian	**39**	**32**	125
	Cambrian	**127**	**75**	162
	East Coast Joint Stock	**56**	**40**	132
	Festiniog	**128**	**75**	163
	Furness	**179**	**100**	183
	Glasgow & South Western	**42**	**33**	126
	Great Central	**73**	**49**	140
	Great Eastern	**72**	**48**	139
	Great Northern	**71**	**48**	139
	Great North of Scotland	**58**	**41**	133
	Great Western	**163**	**92**	176
	Highland	**41**	**33**	126
	Hull and Barnsley	**181**	**101**	184

Coats of Arms (*cont.*)	Lancashire and Yorkshire	**25**	**25**	119
	London Brighton & South Coast	**94**	**59**	149
	London Chatham & Dover	**93**	**59**	148
	London Midland & Scottish	**164**	**92**	177
	London & North Eastern	**165**	**93**	177
	London & North Western	**23**	**24**	118
	London & South Western	**91**	**58**	147
	Midland	**24**	**24**	119
	North British	**40**	**32**	125
	North Eastern	**74**	**49**	140
	North London	**26**	**25**	120
	North Staffordshire	**182**	**101**	184
	Pullman	**166**	**93**	177
	Rhymney	**126**	**74**	162
	Royal Mail	**57**	**41**	132
	Somerset and Dorset	**180**	**100**	183
	South Eastern	**92**	**58**	149
	Taff Vale	**125**	**74**	161
	West Coast Joint Stock	**55**	**40**	131
Dining Cars	Great Northern	**65**	**45**	136
	Great Western	**66**	**45**	136
	London & North Western	**30**	**27**	121
	Midland (third)	**64**	**44**	135
	Midland (joint stock)	**134**	**78**	165
	West Coast Joint Stock	**63**	**44**	135
Dynamometer Cars	Great Western	**87**	**56**	146
	L.M.S. No. 3	**90**	**57**	147
	London & North Western	**89**	**57**	147
	North Eastern	**88**	**56**	146
Locomotives	British Railways 2-6-4T	**178**	**99**	182
	'Clan' 4-6-2	**193**	**108**	189
	'BR9' Crosti Boiler	**193**	**108**	190
	Caledonian: 2-4-0 (1877)	**33**	**29**	123
	4-2-2 No. 123	**12**	**18**	113
	4-6-2 tank	**84**	**54**	144
	'Barochan'	**101**	**63**	152
	Furness 2-2-2 tank	**9**	**17**	112
	Great Central '1020' class 4-4-0	**59**	**42**	133
	4-6-2 tank	**85**	**55**	145
	Pom-Pom 0-6-0	**111**	**68**	156
	Great Northern Stirling 2-2-2	**7**	**16**	111
	Ivatt 4-2-2	**61**	**43**	134
	Great Western *Teign*	**34**	**29**	123
	'Duke' 4-4-0	**77**	**51**	141
	County 4-4-0	**133**	**80**	166
	County 4-6-0	**139**	**81**	167
	'72XX' 2-8-2T	**177**	**99**	182
	Castle 4-6-0	**186**	**103**	186
	King 4-6-0	**187**	**104**	186
	Highland 'Castle' 4-6-0	**79**	**52**	142
	London Brighton & South Coast 2-6-0	**114**	**69**	158
	London Chatham & Dover 0-4-2T	**11**	**18**	113
	London Midland & Scottish 4-6-4 tank	**67**	**46**	137
	Rebuilt 'Claughton'	**147**	**84**	170
	Red streamlined 4-6-2	**161**	**91**	175

Locomotives (*cont.*)	Caprotti Class '5'	**170**	**95**	179
	2-6-4 tank (Fowler)	**175**	**98**	181
	4-6-2 *Princess Elizabeth*	**183**	**102**	185
	Rebuilt 'Scot' (green)	**189**	**105**	187
	London & North Eastern:			
	Silver Link	**159**	**90**	174
	Thompson 'A2' class	**167**	**94**	178
	2-6-2 tank 'Ll'	**176**	**98**	181
	'A3' 4-6-2 (dark blue)	**185**	**103**	185
	London & North Western:			
	Greater Britain	**27**	**26**	120
	Queen Empress	**29**	**27**	121
	4-6-2 tank	**69**	**47**	138
	Webb compound 4-4-0	**75**	**50**	141
	'Experiment' 4-6-0	**99**	**62**	151
	London & South Western:			
	4-2-2-0 No. 720	**49**	**37**	129
	Midland:			
	2-4-0 No. 158A	**32**	**28**	122
	0-4-4 tank	**70**	**47**	138
	0-6-4 tank	**83**	**54**	144
	4-4-0 class '2'	**115**	**70**	158
	Midland & G.N. Joint 2-4-0	**14**	**19**	114
	North British:			
	'Scott' class 4-4-0	**81**	**53**	143
	4-4-2 tank	**86**	**55**	145
	North Eastern:			
	'V' class 4-4-2	**117**	**71**	163
	0-6-0 (Fletcher)	**31**	**28**	122
	North Staffordshire 0-6-2T	**68**	**46**	137
	Southern:			
	Rebuilt 'Nelson'	**149**	**85**	170
	0-6-0 'Q1' class	**168**	**94**	178
	'Schools' (wartime)	**169**	**95**	179
	'Merchant Navy' 4-6-2	**184**	**102**	185
	South Eastern: Cudworth 2-4-0	**13**	**19**	114
	South Eastern & Chatham:			
	'L' class 4-4-0	**47**	**36**	128
	Trevethick's locomotive	**1**	**13**	109
Postal Vans	Great Northern 6-wheel T.P.O.	**108**	**66**	155
	Great Western T.P.O.	**96**	**60**	150
	Great Western 'Ocean Mail' stowage van	**107**	**66**	154
	Highland T.P.O.	**95**	**60**	149
	Midland 6-wheel T.P.O.	**110**	**67**	156
	W.C.J.S. T.P.O. van	**109**	**67**	155
Signals	Brunel's Disc and crossbar	**53–54**	**39**	131
	Distant Arms:			
	Great Western	**144**	**82**	169
	L.B.S.C.R.	**141**	**82**	168
	L.N.W.R.	**142**	**82**	168
	Midland	**143**	**82**	169
	Early, Stewarts Lane	**51–52**	**38**	130
	Gantries:			
	Great Northern	**191**	**106**	188

Signals (*cont.*)	L.N.W.R.	**192**	**107**	188
	Semaphores, main:			
	Caledonian	**104**	**64**	153
	Great Eastern	**103**	**64**	153
	Great Northern	**106**	**65**	154
	North Eastern	**105**	**65**	154
	Semaphore, subsidiary:			
	Great Eastern	**121**	**72**	160
	Great Western	**119**	**72**	160
	Great Western	**124**	**73**	161
	L.B.S.C.R.	**123**	**73**	161
	L.S.W.R.	**120**	**72**	160
	Midland	**122**	**73**	161
	South Eastern & Chatham types	**173–4**	**97**	180
	Tall Posts:			
	Great Western	**145**	**83**	169
	L.N.W.R.	**146**	**83**	169
	Upper Quadrant	**171–2**	**96**	179
Sleeping Cars	East Coast Joint Stock	**35**	**30**	123
	London & South Western Ocean Specials	**38**	**31**	125
	Midland & N.B. Joint	**156**	**88**	173